# BEYOND
## MEDALS OF VALOR

Vietnam Combat Veteran's Life Struggle with Post Traumatic
Stress Disorder (PTSD) and His Adventurous Life Experiences

## BILL ROBERTS

**BALBOA.**
PRESS
A DIVISION OF HAY HOUSE

Balboa Press books may be ordered through booksellers or by contacting:

Balboa Press
A Division of Hay House
1663 Liberty Drive
Bloomington, IN 47403
www.balboapress.com
1-(877) 407-4847

Because of the dynamic nature of the Internet, any web addresses or links contained in this book may have changed since publication and may no longer be valid. The views expressed in this work are solely those of the author and do not necessarily reflect the views of the publisher, and the publisher hereby disclaims any responsibility for them.

The author of this book does not dispense medical advice or prescribe the use of any technique as a form of treatment for physical, emotional, or medical problems without the advice of a physician, either directly or indirectly. The intent of the author is only to offer information of a general nature to help you in your quest for emotional and spiritual well-being. In the event you use any of the information in this book for yourself, which is your constitutional right, the author and the publisher assume no responsibility for your actions.

Any people depicted in stock imagery provided by Thinkstock are models, and such images are being used for illustrative purposes only. Certain stock imagery © Thinkstock.

ISBN: 978-1-4525-7534-6 (sc)
ISBN: 978-1-4525-7536-0 (hc)
ISBN: 978-1-4525-7535-3 (e)

Library of Congress Control Number: 2013910359

Printed in the United States of America.

Balboa Press rev. date: 06/18/2013

GENERAL ORDERS                                        5 April 1968
NUMBER    870

## AWARD OF THE BRONZE STAR MEDAL FOR HEROISM

1.  TC 320.  The following AWARD is announced.

▓▓▓▓▓▓▓▓    FA19888789  ▓▓▓▓▓▓    SPECIALIST FOUR E4 UNITED STATES
ARMY Company C 4th Battalion (Airborne) 503d Infantry

Awarded:  Bronze Star Medal with "V" Device
Date action: 30 January 1968
Theater: Republic of Vietnam
Reason:  For heroism in connection with military operations against a hostile
force:  Specialist Four ▓▓▓▓ distinguished himself by exceptionally
valorous actions on 30 January 1968 in the Republic of Vietnam.  On
this day Company C, 4th Battalion (Airborne), 503d Infantry was engaged
in heavy contact with an estimated enemy battalion well concealed and
fortified in a built up area.  Specialist ▓▓▓▓ was instrumental in
his squad's gaining fire superiority.  He constantly exposed himself
to enemy fire as he moved forward to bring more effective fire upon the
enemy.  When the company withdrew in preparation for air strikes and
artillery, Specialist ▓▓▓▓ volunteered to carry the wounded and dead
to the rear.  He then went forward under the intense automatic weapons
and sniper fire and withdrew several casualties to safety.  Although
under great physical strain from carrying wounded from the front lines
to the evacuation point he showed no sign of discouragement, but continued his difficult task until all wounded were removed.  After this
he returned to the front and continued to fight with his squad.  Specialist Four ▓▓▓▓' outstanding display of aggressiveness, devotion
to duty, and personal bravery were in keeping with the highest traditions of the military service, and reflect great credit upon himself,
his unit, and the United States Army.

Authority:  By direction of the President under the provisions of Executive
order 11046, 24 August 1962 and USARV Message 16695, AVA-S, 1 July
1966.

FOR THE COMMANDER:

OFFICIAL:

KEITH B. WOLFF
Captain, AGC
Assistant Adjutant General

JOHN M BYRNE
Major, AGC
Adjutant General

# DESCRIPTION

Through this book the author, in a very personal way, takes the reader on an amazing feeling-level journey as he stumbles through his life. He talks about his raw gut-wrenching combat experiences as a paratrooper infantryman in Vietnam and what he learned about life along the way.

Bill uniquely contrasts cruelty and death during the war with post-war acts of love and humanitarianism in an effort to save his own life. In this entertaining true story, he deeply explores and unravels his struggle with the insanity of PTSD and his search for truth and meaning. He explains the importance of service to others and, as a college counselor, captures in depth the humorous and serious nature of human behavior and why people behave the way they do. These stories, in all likelihood, have never before been told in this context.

# DEDICATION

This book is dedicated to my wife, Joanne, daughter, Melissa Sanchez, and son, William, who lived with my PTSD problems and took a lot of crap.

It is also dedicated to all those combat veterans and families who are struggling with grief and PTSD—may it help them to find peace.

# ACKNOWLEDGEMENTS

My wife, Joanne: Key loving advisor and clerical assistant.

Melissa Sanchez: Loving support and assistance.

Janie Tate: A sister's feedback at the end of her life.

Mary Snyder: Literary consultant and friend.

Art Ortiz: Inside Photographs.

Rene Sanchez and Chris Apperson: Cover Photo (www.tgavc.com)

# CONTENTS

# FOREWORD

This is my true story as I alone perceive it. My battle experiences are outrageous, with explicit details from a paratrooper infantryman's perspective of the immorality, lies from the top, and insanity of the Vietnam War. The gripping detail of jungle warfare is riveting, touching and raw. I describe my intense search for meaning and my long battle with post-traumatic stress disorder (PTSD) after the war. I detail my college experiences during the turbulent counterculture movement of the sixties, which deeply affected the country and was instrumental in stopping the war.

Recounting my efforts through the years to find myself, I explain the darkest period of my life in the war and its paradoxical connection to my epiphany, a spiritual discovery of service, compassion, and love toward others as a means of preventing my own suicide. I also describe my long journey toward healing. In this book I seek self-forgiveness, forgiveness of others and of God for my stupidity and for my perverse taking of life. I detail my observations of class struggle, both in the military and at my job at a college in California as a professor and counselor and as a director of a large disabled student services program.

I also take the reader through the building and managing of a recreational vehicle (RV) trailer park and the hilarious and tragic adventures of a unique sub-culture that is probably one of the lowest socioeconomic groups in our society. I believe my stories will make the reader, cry, laugh, and become angry at the arrogance of authority and how history continues to repeat itself.

I realized years ago that surviving PTSD meant facing the whole truth. If I can help combat veterans cope with their problems and find truth and meaning in their lives as a result of this book, I will be deeply gratified.

Some names and places have been changed to protect the privacy of the men who fought and of the families of the dead.

Bill Roberts

# - 1 -

# REALLY DUMB KIDS

In 1956, when I was sixteen, I dropped out of high school and worked as a box boy at a small market in the town of Canoga Park, where I grew up. The town, located at the west end of the San Fernando Valley, had not much more than two thousand people. The people took pride in their pristine town with their well-groomed lawns, handsome homes, and fenceless yards, which failed to separate one property from another.

It was a friendly town. As far back as I can remember, the big yearly event was the Christmas parade on Sherman Way Boulevard, which ran about eight blocks through the length of the downtown area. Decorations strung across the boulevard gave off a festive glow. Everyone felt the Christmas spirit, exchanging pleasantries and warm gestures. The townspeople were kind, peaceful, and watched out for each other's children. In fact, whenever I'd get into some sort of mischief, my mother would know about it before I even got home.

Everyone seemed to know each other except for "Handsome Harry," a shell-shocked World War I veteran who kept to himself. He lived in a house surrounded by thick bamboo and rode a bicycle as his main form of transportation. For thrills we kids used to teasingly holler, "Handsome Harry!", and he would chase us on his bicycle with fire in his eyes. We could ride faster and always outran him, but we were still pretty scared.

In elementary school I had my share of troubles. One time I got caught smoking in the top of a high pine tree on the school grounds. My kindergarten teacher spanked me in front of the class. She was a gentle person so it really didn't hurt, but it certainly hurt my pride.

I don't remember much about first grade except that I lived in fear of my teacher, Mrs. Crumb. She was actually a sweet woman, but she probably weighed about three hundred pounds. We sat in tiny chairs in very narrow rows. When she'd walk down the aisles she would almost knock over kids on either side with her big butt as she tried to waddle through.

It was my luck that the boy next to me needed a lot of assistance. Mrs. Crumb would often squeeze through the row, turn to him and bend over his tiny desk to assist him. When she did, more than half the light in the classroom would go dark, and I would feel claustrophobic, consumed by her immense rear end hanging over me. I knew nothing about physics, but I was aware that if she ever lost her balance and fell backwards I was going to be in serious trouble. I dreaded her helping this student, but I didn't complain about it because even at that young age I sensed the mention of my fear would be disrespectful. This would be my cross to bear for that year.

In the fifth grade my teacher was a strict authoritarian. Mr. Foster was mean; he taught by fear and fear alone. One time he took me to the cloak room to hit me with a paddle. He got me in the bent-over position, and I was watching him carefully with my peripheral vision, waiting and scared to death because his punishment was painful. When he reared back to maximize his swing, I got the idea that I would jump in the air just at the perfect time and turn half of a back flip to lessen the impact.

The paddle connected with my butt, my back, and the back of my head at the same time, landing me unhurt on my back on the floor. I played it up by pretending I was unconscious for a few moments. The poor teacher almost had a heart attack thinking I was seriously injured and wondering if his teaching career was over. All he wanted to know was if I was all right. He was badly shaken up. I found out later that he never paddled anyone again. Who knows, maybe that one incident was the beginning of a nation-wide policy to end corporal punishment in public schools. Perhaps I had started a revolution.

There was so little crime that for years we only had one cop on a bicycle who enforced the law. If there was anything serious happening, which I can't recall, the main police in Van Nuys, ten miles away, would respond. Our cop's name was Sam. I remember him as being in his fifties or sixties. He never bothered anyone and mostly just rode around the town. At night he would make sure the doors of the businesses were locked. I can't remember him doing anything else. He didn't seem to be very friendly as I seldom, if ever, saw him stop and talk to people, but I never saw him write a citation, warn, or correct anyone, and I never heard of him arresting anyone. Despite his standoffishness, the townspeople liked him, and everyone felt secure knowing Sam was the law and was on the job.

Not one black person lived in town, and there were only a couple hundred Hispanic people, who confined themselves to two or three square blocks on the other side of town. Canoga Park was surrounded by agricultural areas, which drew the Mexican population there to do the manual work. The Mexican kids went to the public grammar school but were mostly taught in a couple of small bungalows located away from the main school building.

I never saw it as segregation because I never knew what that meant. That was just the way it was, and everybody believed it was right. We were friends with the Mexican kids and played with them during recess. I would often trade my dried-up peanut butter sandwiches for fresh burritos with eggs and beans wrapped in homemade fresh tortillas. They were delicious, and I wondered why they would trade me for my sandwiches. Looking back on it, they were probably just as bored with the same old thing for lunch every day as I was and were eager to have variety.

There was a boy who lived at the end of town whose father was a police officer working in Van Nuys about ten miles away. His uncle was a merchant marine, who in his travels went to China, which was occupied by the Japanese during World War II. Apparently the Japanese considered him to be neutral, as he was free to take photographs.

My friend showed me pictures of soldiers beheading prisoners. He also showed me pictures of people in stocks; they looked like small towers with a hole in the top that held most of a man's weight by his chin and the back of his head, with just his toes on the ground. It took some real evil to think up that contraption of torture. I also saw a picture of a women tied to a post. A soldier was carving off her breasts while looking in her eyes with great interest as he watched her agony.

I remember having bad dreams and thinking, "How could anyone do something that horrible to another person?" I carried that memory along with the fear of something like that happening to me. I carried the realization that there could possibly be some people in my own town who might be capable of doing something like that—maybe someone like Handsome Harry. I still think about those people who were horribly tortured, and I realize the importance of protecting children from pulling up these kinds of horrors on the internet. Those pictures tainted my childhood with fears that a child should never know, but time went on until I turned sixteen.

I came from a family of six kids, with an older brother and sister and three younger siblings. My father, while a good provider, was too busy at work to spend any time with me. My mother gave most of her attention to the oldest and youngest. Being a middle child, I wasn't supervised enough and could do just about anything I wanted without being noticed. Turnig sixteen years old proved to be a major transition point for me because I could buy my own car, have a better job, and be independent and free.

The car was truly my emancipation. Because of my grocery job I had money in my pocket to make an offer of twenty dollars to an old lady who had in her back yard a 1940 Chevy that barely ran. She accepted my offer, making me the proud owner of my very first automobile. All I had to do was replace the spark plugs, and it ran like a new car.

About half a dozen of the kids I grew up with also worked and acquired cars. We all became free spirits, wild and adventurous. We discovered places where we could take our girlfriends; we could party without being bothered by anybody and without bothering anybody else.

We started consuming huge amounts of alcohol bought for us by a couple of people who were over twenty-one. We drank a lot of Thunderbird wine and Country Club malt liquor, and many nights I found myself on somebody's lawn with the dry heaves, thinking I would surely die and even hoping I would. I'd pray and make deals with God that if I could just survive I would never touch alcohol again. That promise was short-lived as the next night I would once again be drinking with my friends. We would vomit out the windows of each other's cars. In fact my car had streaks along the side where stomach acid had eaten away the paint.

We would drive for speed, skidding sideways around corners and racing each other. We knew Sam the cop wouldn't be out that late on his bicycle and would not be able to identify us anyway. A friend and I stole a couple of cars for joyrides just to see if we could get away with it. We also got drunk and went into restaurants wanting to start fights.

One time three of us started a fight that turned into a brawl. I started it by sticking out my foot and tripping a man who was walking by. During the fight we climbed onto the serving counter, where people were eating, using it to jump on people. I was doing very well until I turned around to see a huge fist coming at me about two inches from my face.

I proudly wore a black eye for three weeks, considering it a badge of honor.

After one of our adventures we would drink beer and relive the whole thing, laughing and complimenting each other. We did the wildest and craziest things we could think of because it was a kick in the ass, with alcohol always at the center of what we were doing wrong.

One of our gang was desperately poor. His dad supported seven kids on a janitor's salary, working at the local school. He had one older sister, and the rest were years younger. The little ones, I remember, always had green snotty upper lips. The mother, who was a huge, nonverbal Native American, never wiped their noses. The father was a very nice, hardworking, gentle man who loved his family and who played the harmonica in the evenings.

There was no room for Todd in the tiny house, so he made a room in the old broken-down barn next to the house. On one end of the barn was a small enclosed room with a slab floor, which was once used to keep chickens. Todd used it as his bedroom. It had been cleaned up and furnished with a bed and an old dresser. We used it as a clubhouse where we would meet late at night or when his dad was working. Besides using horrifically foul language and saying terrible things about each other, we smoked cigarettes and involved ourselves in rough play, punching each other in the arms and giving each other charley horses.

Sometimes we would all masturbate with pages of women's underwear torn out of the Sears catalogue. This had nothing to do with homosexuality, as we were all crazy about girls. Instead it was a kind of male bonding experience. Forty years later when I talked to one of the old neighborhood girls on the phone I learned that the girls would sneak over there and watch us through the cracks in the wood. I think the girls told everybody about it. I am still embarrassed. No wonder we weren't very popular or welcome in other people's houses.

My friend Ed used to have us drive him around so he could hang out the window and demolish mailboxes with a baseball bat as we drove by. One time at a party where parents weren't home, the police showed up after one of the neighbors complained. The police accused two of the girls of being prostitutes. I defended their honor and ended up being beaten up by them and spending the night in the drunk tank in Van Nuys—which I deserved. In fact, I was so bad they should have shot me. I was the first one of our group to get arrested, which earned me social status with the other guys.

Shortly afterwards, Ed was drunk and driving recklessly at night when he saw from a distance that a police car was after him. He turned off his lights and started driving through alleys. They caught him and poured out his beer, which is what they usually did. Ed wanted to go to jail. Not only did he resist, he kicked the police car door and begged them to arrest him. They did not arrest him but instead asked him to go home. If you wanted something, the police would never cooperate.

Thank God there were no drugs around at that time in our lives, or I'm sure we would have been heavily involved. We had heard of drugs, but they were far from being accessible to us. We weren't exposed to marijuana until age twenty-one, and by then we were established "juicers."

I dropped out of high school in the eleventh grade so I could work more hours and make more money to support all the fun I was having. My expenses were minimal since I was living at home. After a late night I would sneak in through my bedroom window without making any noise. My parents were too busy trying to take care of the other kids, and they really couldn't control me anyway. Both of my parents were college educated, but for some reason they never stressed to me the importance of education or of individual responsibility. I think they were just too busy trying to make ends meet.

My friends and I were trying hard to achieve what we thought was real manhood. We got the idea from movies that being a man meant that one had to be able to consume huge amounts of alcohol without puking, sometimes act crazy, be physically tough, fearless, and screw anything that moved—except for our girlfriends. A real man had to protect his girlfriend's honor. For the most part my friends and I did not have sex with our girlfriends, because "we loved them too much," as we claimed to them, each other, and ourselves. We respected them and were protective. We were also possessive to the point of a fist fight if someone else showed interest in them.

Tijuana was a little more than a hundred miles away. We would often go there because we could get into all the bars and take full advantage of inexpensive prostitutes. We didn't realize at the time that if you were old enough to climb onto a barstool, you would be served alcohol. We thought we looked old enough, and we used low voices so the bartender would be fooled into thinking we were real men.

We lived in our fantasies and created our own world of entertainment, our own values, morals, and norms, which were a mixture of hedonism, me-first selfishness, irresponsibility, and wild fun at any cost. Paradoxically, we practiced purity and decency when it came to our girlfriends and family.

Ironically, we all came from good homes so there is really no explanation for why we behaved like we did, except for the absence of supervision as well as raging hormones that made us try hard to be manly and cool. I used to wear my hair in a pompadour with so much pomade that on hot days it would run down my face. I wore T-shirts with a pack of Lucky Strike cigarettes rolled up in a sleeve. My shirt was tucked into my Levis, which were pulled down low, and I had horseshoe taps on the heels of my shoes that made a noticeably loud noise when I walked. I remember walking across an intersection once where cars were waiting for the light, believing that everyone was admiring me and thinking that I was so cool. I realize now that they probably were thinking I was a punk who needed the shit slapped out of him.

By today's standards, we didn't do anything that terribly wrong. We may have been suffering from too much time on our hands. I think the leaders of that little town must have known what we were up to and were concerned that we were headed for serious trouble. I believe this because a young man in his twenties (a social worker of sorts) suddenly showed up. It was like he specifically sought us out and started befriending us.

No one knew who he was or where he came from, but we knew he had targeted us. He tried very hard to get to know us and gain our acceptance. We liked him because he seemed to care about us, and we responded in kind. He started organizing social events for us such as backyard get-togethers where we could have some clean fun without alcohol. He arranged some parties, and we had to promise not to bring wine or beer. A couple of times we showed up with alcohol but found ourselves feeling really guilty because this person would break down in tears.

He counseled us and took seriously his efforts to try to help us do the right thing. We didn't have the heart to let him down. He organized us into a softball team, where we could compete in a league against other teams at the park. Before that, we used the park for vandalism and senseless mischief. Now we were all acquiring baseball gloves, rubbing them down with linseed oil, and punching them over and over to form a perfect pocket.

We looked forward to our weekly softball games. I have fond memories of seeing the bugs flying around the lights, the smell of green grass, and the noises of the spectators trying to heckle the pitcher and the batter with chants like, "Hey babe babe babe babe babe," just before the pitch was thrown. I never understood if this was meant to heckle or support, but it added to the excitement and the flavor and culture of the game.

All of us guys were involved in something that we felt was meaningful. Baseball was much more fun than lying in the dark grass with my BB gun, sniping the outfielders in their asses, or throwing a cherry bomb in the gym during a big square dance. My position on the team was centerfield, and I can say with great pride that I never missed a fly ball the whole season. Our social worker, who was our coach, never got angry with us when we made errors, which was all the time. Instead, he somehow taught us to instill in ourselves a feeling of pride and of doing a good job in making some great plays, even though we never won a single game during the entire season. Through his caring and skilled efforts, I believe he saved us from getting into very serious trouble.

I think the serious problems with a lot of our youth today (gangs, drugs, violence, including murders and incarcerations at an early age) could be greatly curtailed if young men and women, like the person who helped my friends and me, would be hired by the thousands to penetrate neighborhoods in trouble all over the country and to begin to break through the culture of crime by providing the same services to them as we received.

I propose that half of NASA's budget be used to hire these special people. Over and over again I have heard that the high cost of our space program goes toward learning about the origins of earth. Although the government has ended the space shuttle program, they are planning to create ways to live on the moon and Mars and to fend off possible threatening asteroids. While I believe this has plenty of merit, it is my belief that we have reached near the end of what we can accomplish in space. The billions of dollars could be used more wisely to create programs for troubled youth, including competitive sports, neighborhood science projects, music, and other educational and creative youth activities. After all, the future of this nation relies on our youth. There are a lot of young, vital, social worker types with plenty of energy and dedication to be able to accomplish this.

As Americans, we need to start focusing more on making breakthroughs here on earth to fashion a better society, ending the destructive forces of violent gangs, drugs, educational problems, and all the other ills that plague us. Helping our youth is far more critical than landing on Mars. Instead of ignoring the problems and not caring as we have for decades, let's do something. I believe we could change the direction of our country by channeling these lost inner-city wayward kids' energies in a positive direction. If we do, there is a good chance we might be able to head off the continuing deterioration of our country.

By looking at it in the long-term, the decline and unraveling of our social fabric over the last fifty years can be seen clearly. If a serious social problem progresses slowly, people don't notice it right away and get used to it. They become desensitized and, in a strange way, even accept it as the way things are. Besides, we have short-sighted planning. We can't think past the next election, and we don't like paying for anything the politicians say is wasteful spending.

Unfortunately, this kind of mass government expenditure to help our youth would go over with most Americans like a lead balloon. In this country there is no value in that kind of thinking. It's every man for himself, rugged individualism, and a passionate aversion to government-sponsored social programs. Given the current political climate, I'm sure these expenditures would never be approved. The excuse has always been that it is the responsibility of churches, schools, volunteer agencies, and families to deal with society's social problems, not the government.

When my little gang became of age, all of us went into the military for more adventure, and we went our separate ways. This was in 1958. A couple of us joined the Navy reserve at age seventeen. If we wore our Navy uniforms we could get into drive-in theaters for free, and the chicks paid attention to us. The Navy reserve required two years of going to meetings every other week, two years of active duty, and two years of standby.

This was a time of peace in our country, between wars, and I thought the military experience was a lot of fun. During my two years of active duty I was stationed on a destroyer tender and had the job of boat coxswain (in charge of a thirty foot utility boat). We traveled to most of the Westpac Asian countries and had a blast. During that time, like most of the other sailors, I was so drunk I can't remember much about it and didn't learn a thing about other countries or cultures. We must have made a terrible impression overseas as we would get drunk, act disrespectfully toward the indigenous people, holler and throw bottles, and, if there was nobody to fight from other ships, we would fight each other.

Whenever we had liberty, I couldn't get past the first bar. I prided myself on being a real partier and was not serious about anything except my girlfriend back home. I thought I loved her deeply and saw her as my teenage goddess. After my stint in the Navy I planned to get a job, make something of myself, and marry her. I noticed, however, near the end of my sea duty, that she wasn't writing. I heard that she had moved away from Canoga Park, had gotten a job, and lived in Laguna Beach.

Immediately after I got out of the Navy, I contacted her, and she invited me to come to dinner at her apartment. I showed up with beer and wine, ready to have a romantic evening. She introduced me to a guy who would be with us for dinner. I didn't know what to make of it until she made the announcement that they were getting married. She said she loved us both and that it was a hard decision for her. I thought at first that I should jump up and beat the shit out of the guy, but he was too big. I was so shocked and devastated that I just got up, walked out to my car, and drove off.

Thinking about it later, I understood that her choice was probably correct. He possessed a two-year associates degree and was a hot insurance salesman, while I was just a crazy, drunken loser who had dropped out of high school. Even understanding that, I thought that I could not live without her, as she was the young sexy goddess of my dreams. What would I do without her?

# - 2 -

# CANOGA PARK AND SPUTNIK

At that time, not too long after the Russians had sent Sputnik into orbit, Canoga Park changed forever. Defense plants were popping up all over town, and there were hundreds of tract homes being built all over the outskirts of town to accommodate the influx of people working in these plants. Even though I was a high school dropout loser, I was hired after a two-minute interview to work at a place called Atomics International.

With no training, I was dressed in boots made of cloth and a white lab coat with a film badge that would detect if I received too much radiation. In a few weeks I would receive a security clearance. I learned later that the FBI had interviewed my friends at this bar I frequented called the Wiggie Room Beer Tavern. Despite having dropped out of school and having no real references other than the Navy, I was hired to work in the metallurgy lab as a technician, as if I knew what I was doing.

They were hiring people like me right off the street. Several other no-talents I knew had also been hired. I soon caught on to what I was supposed to do, and, despite sometimes nipping a little industrial alcohol in the lab, I actually did a decent job, or at least I thought I did. My job was to prepare samples of fuel rods and other metals and to photograph them under a microscope to be examined by engineers.

The purpose of Atomics International (AI) was to build a small reactor called SNAP which would be used in space to generate electricity. I never did learn what "SNAP" meant.

I found out later that they had a working reactor that was actually providing electricity to a portion of the community and that supposedly nobody knew about it. This information came from my friend's uncle, who was employed there as an engineer.

This was the best job I ever had so far, and I had a lot of fun. One time on a slow day I was screwing around with a giant press. I was alone in the room. I had been pressing different kinds of metal together in the beginning stages of making fuel rods. I decided I would press a fifty-cent piece to increase greatly the diameter of the coin. I thought it would make a good conversation piece. With this press you had to release the pressure slowly, because a sudden release of fifty-thousand pounds would sound like an explosion.

I put the coin between two dies and cranked up the pressure to the max. Before I could let the pressure off, the dies broke, causing a loud explosion. Alarms started going off all over the building, and everyone was ordered to evacuate. I gathered up the pieces immediately and put them in my pocket. I didn't care that they might have been radioactive; I just wanted to get rid of the evidence. I filed out with everyone, who were all asking each other what could have happened. I looked just as curious and worried as everyone else. I was never caught and never told anyone.

After a few years of having plenty of beer money and security, suddenly, out of nowhere, the whole reactor project was canceled. Most everyone was laid off, and the entire plant closed down. It was a shocker—I thought I would work there with my lab coat, screwing around for the rest of my life. The thought did cross my mind that maybe I had something to do with it closing down. I couldn't believe the money the government spent during those years, only to shut the place down. My job paid a decent wage, which I squandered in the Wiggie Room, building up my bar tabs, paying rent for my little apartment, and making motorcycle payments.

After that, I started working in landscaping, digging trenches in the hot sun. The easy life was over, and, as a diversion, I became a member of the shuffleboard team at the Wiggie Room.

# - 3 -

# SEEING GOD

Shuffleboard is a game played on a narrow wooden table about twenty feet long. Shuffleboard was big in the early 1960s, even bigger than pool. I am surprised it wasn't covered on television nor had national recognition. Every beer tavern had a shuffleboard table and its own team. We played in an organized league consisting of about twenty bars.

For a couple of years, the Wiggie Room was in first place. We all received numerous trophies over a foot high with a little shuffleboard table on top. I had at least half a dozen of these large trophies, which later on would mean nothing. Seemingly overnight the game had lost its popularity, and nobody knew what the hell it was. I thought at the time that the trophies were very meaningful because in my own mind they depicted extremely gifted and accomplished athletes. People who won national stock car races didn't have trophies as big as mine, which I proudly displayed on my windowsill at my apartment.

I closed up the bar at two a.m. every night and drove home very drunk like a crazy person on my motorcycle. My motorcycle was a 1963 Triumph 650 TT Special. It was a lightweight, cut down model dirt bike that didn't even have a battery. The literature on it said it had been tested at 100 mph in a quarter of a mile, which was fast in those days. Riding my motorcycle gave me the feeling of total freedom. It was a miracle that I was not killed, because I loved to accelerate and go at top speeds through windy canyon roads.

After I had been laid off from my lab job and had collected unemployment for a while, I was working part-time for a landscaping company while continuing to enjoy reckless adventures. I tried motorcycle racing and bull riding, but I wasn't good at either. I got mixed up briefly in a love triangle and almost got shot. Hanging around a lot of disturbed people in bars lends itself to possible dangers.

There was a cocktail lounge across from the Wiggie Room parking lot where my drinking partner and I often went when we were through with shuffleboard. Already about sixteen beers in, we would have a few nightcaps before going home. We liked the owner, who would give us an occasional drink on the house.

We also liked to watch the topless naked Watusi dancer perform on an elevated platform. We would act cool and disinterested even though our hearts were jumping out of our chests. It was fun to observe others acting cool but literally drooling from their mouths and trying to hide the erections in their pants.

One time the owner's wife showed up with another man, and they sat on bar stools directly in front of him across the bar. Everyone noticed and the bar got quiet. She looked at her husband with a sneer that communicated, "I hope you are suffering right now." The man she was with looked at her husband with a look of superiority, which conveyed, "I'm screwing your wife and there is not a thing you can do about it."

Suddenly the owner reached under the bar, pulled out a .38 revolver, and, at point blank range, started shooting at them. My friend and I were the first ones out the back door. The whole bar emptied out faster than a fire drill. I thought I had just witnessed a murder until his wife and her boyfriend ran out the door and took off in the car. She was crying, and he was white as a ghost. Everyone was amazed that the drunken bartender had missed them with all six shots. At that point, everyone went back into the bar, now filled with gun smoke, found their drinks, and things kind of returned to normal. I never understood why the police never came.

One night we observed two men stealing a set of Texas longhorns off the wall and putting them in their truck. They returned to the crowded bar proud of themselves and thinking they had gotten away with it. My friend and I saw what they did and decided to go outside, find the truck with the horns, steal them back, lock them in my friend's car, and give them back to the owner later on. After all, we were loyal to the owner and thought we might get a couple of free drinks out of the deal.

We returned to the bar feeling proud of ourselves, thinking we had done the owner a favor. The two men who stole the horns figured out what we had done and walked up behind us as we sat at the bar. One of them poked us on the shoulder. We turned around on the bar stools to see two very angry men. One of them was about six feet five inches tall and built like a refrigerator. The other man was average height, muscular, and dressed like a cowboy.

The bigger man told us that we were about to meet God; that they were going to annihilate us. My friend and I looked at each other in horror and nonverbally acknowledged that we were indeed about to meet God and there was no way out of it. Regardless, we thought our chances for survival might be better outside. My friend told them, "Okay, why don't we go outside?" They agreed, and we started for the door leading to the back parking lot.

When we got outside and turned around, the huge man threw a punch at my friend but missed. The other cowboy that was going to kill me got distracted momentarily by this missed haymaker punch that could have knocked an automobile on its side. I was in survival mode and took advantage of this distraction: I wound up and punched the cowboy as hard as I could with my own haymaker. It was a lucky punch, and I felt a solid shock wave travel from my fist to my feet. The cowboy fell backwards and hit his head hard on the asphalt. He lay motionless.

I then watched as this giant of a man, now in a rage, threw punch after punch at my friend, who was very quick and agile. He dodged and weaved and ran around backwards avoiding being hit or grabbed by this huge man, who could have easily mangled him with his strength. The big man was totally frustrated and continued giving his all to hurt my friend.

After a couple of minutes he became exhausted, defenseless, and harmless. At that point my friend went after him and cut him down like a big tree. Hell, this was like a fancy fight scene that you would see in a movie. My friend and I thought a miracle had occurred as we both ran to our vehicles and took off before the police arrived. After that we were afraid to frequent that bar again. I was worried that the man I hit may have died or ended up with permanent brain damage when his head hit the blacktop that hard.

It was then that I realized I was going downhill and for sure wasn't going anywhere in my life. I realized also that I was majorly unhappy. I truly didn't care about my life and I knew I had to make a drastic change to pull myself out of this hole I had dug. I was also perforated with guilt knowing that my mother was very worried and disappointed in me. I remember reading a book called *Green Beret*. It was 1965, and I decided to do something with my life that was worthwhile, respectable, and patriotic. Something I could do that my friends and loved ones would be proud of. The Vietnam War was accelerating, and I decided to join the Army.

# - 4 -

# AMERICAN CULTURE AND THE VIETNAM WAR

A merica loves wars. We have had a war every decade for God knows how long. War was an opportunity for young men to prove themselves. Throughout history it was the greatest adventure a young man could pursue. The glory of war was reinforced by war movies and cowboy movies. When I was growing up, there were clearly the bad guys and the patriotic, brave, and morally right good guys.

I wanted this adventure and to be a part of something extremely meaningful. Just thinking about it choked me up, my chest swelling with pride. The sound of march music in my ears was deafening. I decided to join the Army. I never cared about the risk of dying because I had lost my goddess, and I didn't care what happened to me.

Also, like most people, I was alienated from the true reality of war. After a lifelong process of internalizing the great tradition of the American soldier and war, I was anxious to join; I didn't know why I hadn't thought about it sooner. Suddenly, as if overnight, I felt good about myself. My plan was to volunteer for all the danger I could get my hands on. I was promised by the recruiter that if I was "Man enough" I could become a paratrooper, be in the infantry, and go directly to Vietnam. I would be fighting for the most important thing of all, to protect my country and be individually instrumental in stopping any more dominos from falling, as was the theory, where country after country including America could fall to Communism.

God! What an incredibly worthy and noble cause! I couldn't wait to be placed right into the middle of war in real combat. Metaphorically, I had a huge erection in anticipation. I was ready. Oh God, was I ready!

# - 5 -

# VIETNAM

Our 173rd Brigade Company had reached its harbor site for the night, after a ten kilometer (six mile) hump through the rotten jungles over the central highlands near the Cambodian border. In a small open area protected by thick jungle, the company (about ninety men) formed their perimeter. The perimeter was usually about seventy-five to one hundred feet in diameter. Defensive positions had been dug, and all of us grunts were settled in for another night in paradise.

It was not my squad's turn to go out and set up an ambush, and so we would remain with the company that night. Defensive fighting positions were dug around the perimeter in case of an attack. Our fighting position consisted of a hole burrowed about chest deep and six feet long. Hand grenades neatly lined the front of the position, where they were easy to feel and locate in the dark and had their pins straightened for easy removal. Two Claymore mine detonators, called "clickers", were on each side of the position. Ammunition bags containing M16 magazines were also at reach.

About twenty-five feet to the front of the position, trip flares and their wires had been strung out, which would light up the place if someone were to walk through. Approximately halfway between our position and the flares, Claymore mines would provide an eighty ball-bearing, horizontal directional blast like great shotguns in the event we were overrun.

Behind our position, our hooches, made of two ponchos tied together and draped over a three-foot high frame made of branches, provided shelter from the rain. The hooch would hold three strong one-man air mattresses, which would keep our bodies off the wet ground. We had one hour of stand-to at dusk and at dawn when the enemy was most likely to attack. The whole company would be ready for battle at those times. After dusk we would eat our C-Rations, which would soon be transformed into diarrhea.

It would be my turn first to guard the position while the others slept. I sat on my steel pot helmet by the position, which had already begun to fill with water. I had smeared myself with insect repellent in an effort to discourage mosquitoes and leeches from getting on me. I draped my rotten poncho liner (small blanket), which smelled like filthy socks, over my shoulders for protection against the night chill. I was aware of every noise and would analyze these noises for possible enemy movement.

I had learned to analyze noises even in my sleep. I was especially alert as the night before we had gotten into a hand grenade throwing contest with the local Viet Cong (VC) that had wounded a few people in the company who had to be 'dusted off' (medically evacuated) the next morning. We never knew when we would be attacked at night. We threw grenades at first because firing weapons would give away

27

our exact location. We had to be careful throwing grenades because they could easily hit a tree and bounce back.

We knew that the enemy knew where we were. Would we get hit again? Would we be mortared? Would we be attacked and overrun by the hard-core North Vietnam Army (NVA)? Would I die tonight? All I knew was that for the moment things were okay.

I thought about my goddess who had dumped my loser ass and who was probably snuggled up to her husband in a nice, warm, comfortable bed after a romantic dinner and lovemaking. I felt alone and heartsick. I longed for her but to no avail.

I was exhausted but aware of the relief of not having my eighty to one hundred pound rucksack tearing away at my shoulders, and the burning and itching of ant bites and jungle rot, which I would ask the doctor to painfully scrub and bandage the next morning. I was aware of my stench, having not bathed or changed clothes for a week. Most of all, I was aware of my expendability and the big question: Could I survive a year of this shit knowing that about one-third of us would die during our tour of duty?

In the beginning of my army experience in the states, I found relationships to be very unordinary compared to civilian life. What seemed wrong to me was seeing a twenty-one-year-old lieutenant make a career sergeant, who was old enough to be his father, stand at attention while chewing his ass up one side and down the other like a young boy in military school. I guess that is the way the authority hierarchy had to work, but there was just something wrong with that picture.

What I did not like was the dichotomy between officers and enlisted men in general. I think I came as close as possible to understanding how black people must have felt in the South in the fifties and sixties. Enlisted men seemed to be looked down upon greatly by officers, not respected, nor appreciated, discriminated against in terms of their legal and human rights, and stereotyped for the most part as dumb, warm bodies.

It was like the whole military was set up for officers. They received twice the amount of parachute jump pay, twice the amount of combat pay, and they only had to spend six months in the field compared to our one year. I suspect the officers received more R & R time than we did also. Back in the states their officers' clubs and living quarters were lavish compared to enlisted men's clubs and living quarters, and they ate better food in an officers' dining room. The higher the officer's rank, the more godlike they became. I wouldn't be surprised if enlisted men were their janitors and their house cleaners on many of the bases in the country. All of this stands to reason because officers were educated and were the leaders.

I guess the system had to work that way. What I really objected to was the fact that they treated enlisted men as whipping boys, as truly second-class citizens. In general, we were regarded as total imbeciles, like shit. We were humiliated and mistreated by most officers on a constant basis, which I think had to affect the whole operation, not to mention affecting how enlisted men felt about themselves. This manifested itself in everybody hating each other, or at least in a major way, not caring. Most soldiers found their own support systems among their own squads (nine to twelve men) and from some of their platoon members (thirty to forty-five men).

Out of all the different military organizations, army people treat each other the worst. I am pretty sure that if suicide rates among different military organizations were studied, the findings would be much higher for people in the army, especially during and after war. That's my opinion based on my experiences.

The recruiter promised me that if I enlisted I would easily become a paratrooper in the infantry and be sent to Vietnam. Since almost everyone did not want to go, it was a sure deal. After basic training, almost everybody received their orders to go to advanced infantry training, so I would volunteer for jump school. However, my orders said that I would report to some army base in the South to be trained for telephone and switchboard repair school. Of course, my reaction was anger. I wanted to be in the infantry. It seemed that, in the army, whatever people wanted they didn't get.

I complained to the company commander in basic training, and he just said there was nothing he could do about it and that I should go ahead and finish the training and then apply for the infantry. My plan was to flunk out of the training, which I thought would put me right in the infantry. Looking into the matter, I found out that if I did flunk out I would be placed in cook's school, and nobody flunks out of cook school. Hell, I already knew that by the taste of the food.

I went ahead and finished the course in switchboard and telephone repair and immediately volunteered for jump school. I was transferred to Fort Benning, Georgia, and completed the three-week volunteer jump school, which ended with five actual jumps from an aircraft. In jump school the training was physically difficult, but since it was considered dangerous and difficult you could quit any time you wanted. The fact that it was voluntary put a whole new and different twist on it, and I felt challenged to complete the school. The static line jumps gave me the sensation of being a small piece of paper thrown out the window of a speeding car, and although it was a little scary, I loved it.

After jump school I went to the company commander and told him of my situation. He said it would be impossible because the army had already trained to me to be a repair man. At that time, I got orders to report to Fort Bragg, home of the airborne in North Carolina. I again went to the officer in charge and asked to be transferred to Vietnam. They needed people in Vietnam, and I was granted my request. In Vietnam I was sent to the 173rd Airborne Brigade and was stationed at the rear area headquarters in a tent, repairing telephones and switchboards.

Obviously, I was really unhappy about the whole situation and decided to follow the chain of command and go as far as I needed to be placed in the infantry. I started with the sergeant in charge of me. His reaction was laughter. I explained that I had a right to follow the chain of command for my request to transfer. He got pretty angry with me but had to send me to the first sergeant of my unit, who also laughed at me and got angry. He said there was no way in hell that I would get my request to go into the infantry. I insisted and was sent to the company commander, who was the rank of captain. He was angry at my request and said no one that he knew had ever done that before and that it would be impossible for me to achieve. But he knew he had to grant me my request to see the next officer higher up.

I then applied to the next officer at the battalion level. I was then able to see the lieutenant colonel and then the colonel. I was then reluctantly, and with great anger toward me, approved to see the man second in charge of the whole 173rd Brigade. It turned out that he was very easy to talk with, and after hearing my story he kind of understood what I wanted. He asked me at the end of my interview, if he couldn't help me, did I plan on seeing the general in charge of the whole brigade. I said, "Yes, sir," and he dismissed me back to the telephone repair tent. In a couple of days I received orders to transfer to an infantry unit.

When I got to my company headquarters they equipped me with all the essentials I needed for the field and put me on a helicopter to be flown to the jungle and our area of operation. I was elated, finally reaching where I wanted to be. I had traded my toolbox for an eighty to one-hundred pound backpack and an M16.

# - 6 -

# BITCH VINES AND BEAUTY IN THE JUNGLE

After about a week of total exhaustion, I started to be physically conditioned to carry the weight and be able to march all day in over one hundred degree heat and one hundred percent humidity. I was soon operating with my squad of nine men in the normal duties of "search and destroy," and I soon fit in as one of the regular "boonie rats." I was taught the tricks of the trade by my squad and by my squad leader sergeant. I was functioning efficiently but had not yet proven myself in combat. It was on-the-job training in guerrilla warfare, and I was told to forget everything I had learned about conventional warfare in basic training back in the States.

Although the beauty of the jungle was breathtaking, it was a dangerous and hostile place. Education about it from my squad was critical for my survival. Perspiration in that kind of heat and humidity was profuse. We had to use water purification tablets and take salt tablets and drink over a gallon and a half of water a day. Water in the jungle was readily available during the wet season, and a little trickier to find during the dry season.

The jungle was so thick in places it was impenetrable. Sometimes we ran into massive configurations of vines that were eight to ten inches in diameter. Some thorns were as big as daggers and so sharp that just a slight pressure against them would pierce your skin. Rains during the monsoon season were so driving that one could soap up and rinse like you were taking a shower back in the States.

Some vines grew long and hung high from trees. Sometimes we swung on them like in the Tarzan movies, as they could easily support our weight. There were small, tough-as-wire vines everywhere, and they were given names by the grunts. We called one vine the "Go to Hell Vine." It ran along the ground a couple of inches high and would often catch your toe, landing you right on your face.

The other and most aggravating vine was called the "Wait a Minute Vine," which would catch in your equipment and hold you back as you were straggling to make headway. Instead of stopping, moving back, and twisting a little to get untangled, new men would become frustrated and in a rage, try to tear their way through with their weight, causing them to be exhausted in a very short time. There were the additional dangers of making unnecessary noise while tearing one's way through the vines, and of conceivably pulling the pin out of a grenade attached to the ammo harness.

There were wasps in groups of about ten that would fly into a man's face, stinging him and knocking him to the ground with him screaming in pain. That never happened to me, but it did happen to a man in front of me and a man behind me. There were ants an inch long that some say could flatten your air mattress. They would sometimes fall down your back and neck, stinging the hell out of you as you brushed under low branches. There were mosquitoes that could easily bite through your clothing and that could cause malaria if we didn't take our daily dose of pills given by the medic each morning.

Leeches would find a way through your clothing, or they would get on your exposed neck, sucking your blood until they were nice and fat and then drop off, leaving a bleeding sore. You couldn't feel them at the time. At night while we were sleeping, the leeches would attack. Many times I got up in the morning and while taking a leak, noticed a bunch of blood in my crotch area where a leech had sneaked in through my fly and attached itself to my genitals.

One morning, my squad leader got up with one hanging out of his nostril, which caused a good, quiet laugh. The leeches were slimy and impossible to pull off your skin. You got them off by burning them or putting a little insect repellent right where they were connected. Sometimes in wet areas where we were stopped, we could see leeches coming toward us, having sensed our presence. We would try to step on them, but they just kept coming. We could not kill them. Insect repellant was our only defense.

The bacteria was so abundant in the rotting jungle that a simple scratch on your skin could turn into a swollen, oozing infection (jungle rot), which would have to be scrubbed with disinfectant and a stiff brush, and then bandaged by "Doc," the medic. It seemed like half of the company walked around with bandages on their arms.

There were water buffalo in the villages that children would lead around by a ring through their noses. The buffalo would sometimes charge at us grunts. We refrained from shooting them because these animals were important to the villagers for their survival. Two varieties of extremely poisonous snakes lived in the jungle also. One was the king cobra, which I never saw, and the other was called the bamboo viper, which we often stepped over, being hidden in the underbrush as we were marching along. The bamboo vipers were a florescent green, about two and a half feet long. I stepped over many of them when it was my turn to walk point. It would be discovered a few men back as the brush was trampled down, and someone would kill it with a machete.

I remember one man was bitten by a bamboo viper and survived thanks to Doc's immediate action of carving away, with a scalpel, a large piece of flesh around the location of the bite. The man yelled out briefly, and then his eyes rolled back in his head. We then called in a med-evac, after cutting a hole in the jungle canopy so the chopper could land. The soldier who got bitten was back in the company about a month and a half later, and received the nickname "Jake the Snake."

The combination of all the bacteria, the water purification tablets, and the malaria pills made for constantly loose stools. It was not uncommon during a physical strain to lose control down your legs and into your boots. We just had to keep marching anyway.

Aside from the harshness of the jungle, there was the raw beauty of lush forests and beautiful tropical plants. There were waterfalls and wild fruits. Rivers of glass slipped along colored rocks under sunrays piercing through the jungle canopy. The birds possessed a marked beauty; even the insects were colorful. There was a giant spider about seven inches in diameter that spun webs large enough, so it seemed, to be able to catch birds. On occasion, we would spot apes swinging from the trees above us. A couple of times when I was walking point, I saw orangutans swing over the top of us, looking down with curiosity. I was told that they were supposed to be extinct in this area of the world.

Once when our company had stopped marching for a few minutes, I noticed that what I was leaning against was an old rock wall. As I looked around, I could see that the whole area had at one time been terraced. I could barely make out what I thought were ancient ruins and structures grown over by thick foliage. Vietnam was ripe for archaeological and anthropological studies, but these areas had been war-torn for thirty years and probably longer. In all probability, no one had been able to get in there to do research.

# - 7 -

# DEADLY BOOBY TRAP

When I first got to the unit, I did not see any action for about two weeks. I felt confident and bold. I was overwhelmed with patriotism, and I felt that saving our country from the spread of communism was the most important work anyone could do. At that time, we were working in an interesting kind of flat terrain. We would run across an occasional hole or bunker, throw in a grenade, and be on our way. For some reason it wasn't our company's policy to do "tunnel rat" work. Just a few feet inside one of the holes we found a dead woman. She was well decomposed, and appeared to be forty or fifty years old. I wondered what her life must have been like, and what led to her death. Had she been a mother and raised a family? What she was now was just a dead body that no one even bothered to bury.

One day we were on a platoon-sized (about thirty men) patrol when we came upon an area where people had been living. They lived in hooches, which were very small, grass-covered structures. We were ransacking them and burning them when I remembered reading about watching carefully for booby traps. Somebody in the squad yelled, "Hey lieutenant, what do you want to do with this pumpkin patch over here?" The lieutenant came over to see. He was a young, easy-going man, and everyone liked him, unlike most of the other officers. His fiancée used to send cookies in her packages from the states, not only just to him but to the whole platoon.

The pumpkin patch consisted of about eight to ten large, green pumpkins or some sort of squash. About half a dozen of us were standing around the patch. The lieutenant walked over and kicked one of them, resulting in a big flash and a tremendous explosion, knocking all of us to the ground. The pumpkin had apparently been hollowed out and booby-trapped, possibly with a mortar round. Six of us standing around the patch had been hit by shrapnel, and most had been seriously wounded.

The lieutenant absorbed almost all of the blast. His arms and legs looked like hamburger, and it looked like his eyes were blown out. He had huge holes in his chest. I never knew a man could bleed that much. The lieutenant was yelling, "My eyes! My eyes!" Then he started yelling that he could not breathe. The medic had arrived and was trying in vain to stop the bleeding. The lieutenant, in the midst of his agony, was in a panic and unable to talk any more. He turned gray and died. It was terrible. The dust off had arrived, and the wounded were flown out first. Soon the helicopter returned to pick up the body. I carried his shredded, blood-soaked shirt to the helicopter. It was very heavy, like a shirt taken out of the washer that had not been spun dry.

It got really quiet; everybody was in a state of shock. We dug in fighting positions and quickly prepared a harbor site ready for the night. Not a word was said all evening. This experience was very serious. I had never fully realized that the enemy was out to kill us just as surely as we were out to kill them. While I expected combat to be ugly, I was now living in the total reality of it. I had been blasted right out of my fantasy as to how I thought war would be.

The night was still. I felt sick to my stomach and could not eat. There was an absence of patriotism, and drum music was not ringing in my ears like before. I still had the strong smell of the lieutenant's blood in my nostrils. I trembled all night long, and I felt a deep sadness as I thought about his family and his fiancée and the terrible suffering they would soon be going through. I understood for the first time the high price of war. I felt an icy contrast between where my head was before the lieutenant's death, and my sudden awareness of the reality of war.

It was a period of insanity for me. I knew I wasn't the only one in shock, as nobody said a word all night long. Several times during the night, I thought I heard muffled sobbing. I couldn't distinguish if it was coming from me or others around me. I felt scared, vulnerable, and cowardly, which I had never felt before and had no control over. I thought over and over again about the fantasy world I had been living in all my life. How could I have thought that any part of this was good? I was deeply sad and confused.

# - 8 -

# TET OFFENSIVE

The next two weeks I tried not to think about the lieutenant. We were operating a few miles west of the city of Tuy Hoa and running into fresh, well-traveled trails. It was scary because the well-traveled trails were indicative of large numbers of the North Vietnamese Army (NVA). Everybody was scared as hell. So much for marching music and patriotism. All of that had been replaced by shitting in my pants.

The next day we quietly walked through three large NVA base camps that were recently emptied out. Where were they? Hundreds of NVA had just been there; you could still smell them. In one of the base camps there was a dirt bank about eight feet high above me with a severed head stuck onto a stick looking down at me. One man on the bank kicked it in my direction, and it rolled down the bank toward my feet. I could hear the brains sloshing inside the skull, and it smelled terrible. Obviously, this man had been some sort of a prisoner who had been executed.

The next night, the distant sky lit up with hundreds of tracer rounds ricocheting into the low cloud cover, and there was a roar of gunfire and explosions that continued into the night. Whatever was going on out there, we knew was big. It was obvious where the NVA in the empty base camps had gone. We later learned that this was the start of the 1968 Tet Offensive, where every major city in Vietnam would be under attack.

The next morning we were flown out of the jungle to the downtown area of Tuy Hoa where all the firing had taken place. We flew in large Chinooks; each double-bladed helicopter held a platoon. We were dropped off in between two villages on the outskirts of town. In between the two villages was a huge sand hill, about thirty feet high and a little more than half a football field long. Nobody had briefed us about what exactly was going on, as they always kept us ignorant and in the dark.

We were then told we were going into the village to destroy a few snipers. We knew it was just another lie, because of all the fire the night before. We heard later that another company had entered the village the night before and had lost eighteen men, plus dozens wounded. I didn't know if it was true or not. There was a battalion of NVA (over three hundred and fifty) built up and well-fortified in that village.

Whoever was directing the assault did not inform us of this; no communication ever came down to us unimportant people. I felt violated. I think that since we were expected to assault the enemy and many of us would be dying, it would have been nice for them to wish us good luck or something. I always had the feeling that we enlisted men were thought of as expendable dumb-asses. I overheard a lieutenant many times in the company referring to us enlisted men as a bunch of duds. I remember thinking at the time how good it would feel to hit him in the face with the butt of my M16. I am sure others shared my fantasy.

The night before, when we heard the battle and saw the tracers in the distance, we assumed that the South Vietnam forces, South Vietnamese Army, and Korean forces had pushed them back and surrounded them in this small village about one hundred yards in diameter. When we arrived, a helicopter was flying over the village, dropping leaflets and using a loudspeaker trying to talk them into surrendering.

The leaflets said that they would be treated well if they surrendered, and they would be reeducated. They were told that it was their last chance to surrender or they would be killed. Of course at the time we couldn't read the leaflets or understand what was being said from the aircraft over the speaker. We assumed that was what the helicopter was all about. I remember wondering at the time why they would go through all of that effort just to get a few snipers to give up. I knew it had to be bigger than that.

Our company was ordered to move up squads abreast and wait about fifty yards from the village ahead that contained the NVA. To the left front was a sand hill. Then we got the order to move forward into the village and assault. I had a bad feeling about what we were about to encounter.

We were about three feet apart as we walked toward the village side by side. Instead of the enemy waiting for us to get close to them, they opened up on us. We were right out in the open. It was like all hell broke loose. We hit the ground and lay as flat as we could while bullets kicked dirt and dust all around us and whizzed over our heads.

People started yelling, "Go to the sand hill to the left!", and we all got up and started running. We had to do something because we were right out in the open with no cover. We ran to the top of the sand hill and positioned ourselves on the rim overlooking the village, which was less than sixty yards away, and we immediately started returning fire.

We could see a lot of NVA running around repositioning their machine guns. There were lots of targets, and we were laying down a lot of fire. Our company commander was also on the sand hill and had been standing up as if he were a cop directing traffic, which was a crazy thing to do because he was cut down right away by enemy fire. I was scared to death and continued to fire and reload as fast as I could, like everyone else, while enemy bullets hit all around us with loud pops and with sand blasting in our eyes.

It wasn't long before people were yelling for a medic. John, who was next to me four feet away, jerked violently and flipped over on his back. He yelled shockingly, "God damn!" His eyes rolled back in his head, and he lay on the sand convulsing. He had been shot in the middle of the chest long ways because of the position of his body. I started yelling, as did the person on the other side of him, for a medic. I knew it would take a while before the medic would come because people all over were being hit. John stopped breathing and died.

He was a genuinely nice person. I hadn't known him long, but we had become close. At night we talked about how it was at home, about girlfriends, hot showers, dreams, ice cream and hamburgers, family, and about our survival, in an effort to cope with the situation we were in. John was the pace counter for our squad, and he always carried a shovel on top of everything else we had to carry, which nobody else wanted to do. The pace counter worked out how many paces it took to equal one meter. Most of the time three paces in the jungle equaled one meter. The purpose was to know how far we had traveled on the map, because in those days there was no such thing as a GPS.

I always speculated that he had some sort of disability, because he had some trouble talking. Everybody loved John. He always tried to do more than his share of whatever work needed to be done. Now he lay dead, and his family didn't even know.

I started to think more about the wounded than I did about the fighting. The person behind us about twelve feet away took a round right through the head, dying instantly. About twenty feet to my right, men were yelling for help.

One man had been shot several times; he was in the open and was continuing to be shot. He needed help and needed to be carried to the evacuation point, a distance away parallel to the battle line, through an open area, to the dust off location. It was suicide to help him. The man who had been shot was in agony and in the open. I was overwhelmed by his suffering. People were yelling for volunteers to help. My mind stopped thinking, and I got up and ran to him. Three other men joined. We rolled him onto a poncho, and each of us grabbed a corner and headed off to the helicopter. We must have carried him over a hundred yards parallel to the enemy while bullets zipped by all around us the entire distance.

It was a long hundred yards, and I couldn't believe we weren't hit. We got to the evacuation point. The helicopter was coming in, and we had to get the man over a four foot barbed-wire fence. Right beside us on the other side of the fence, three high-ranking officers were huddled in a ditch. They were in there watching the battle, I think, so they could later write each other up for medals. Maybe they were directing the battle, but I don't think so. I didn't have time to have a big conversation about it.

We immediately asked them to help this man over the fence. There were lots of rounds still flying all around as those officers sat there. I think they were too afraid to move. I started yelling profanities and ordering them to get their asses up and help the man over the fence. I guess I must have shamed them enough, because they did get up to help the man.

We went back a couple more times to repeat what we had done. I was so stressed out that I have very little memory of doing it. All I know is that later on I would receive a Bronze Star for heroism in ground combat, along with a few others. I would bet that those three high-ranking officers observing the battle probably put each other in for very high medals afterward; that's just the way it was done. I believed there were other men also removing the wounded, so I decided to get back to my squad and help them fight. Besides, I don't think any of us had the strength to continue carrying the wounded.

When I got to my squad I realized my M16 was full of sand and would not fire. Lying on my back, I took my weapon apart. Putting the parts on my chest, I cleaned them with my bottle of insect repellent, which I always kept attached to my helmet band. The battle was beginning to slow down, and at one point we were able to go over to where we had dropped our rucksacks and bring back a little food and water. I had never been so thirsty in my life. During the battle we had been supplied with plenty of ammunition but not food or water. I don't know who brought us the ammunition during the battle, as I have no memory of that.

We were told to "dig in," as we were to remain there through the night. During the battle we had shit all over us; it was on my face from crawling around on my stomach. I don't know if the other men had shit on their faces, but I did. We didn't have a discussion about it because there were more important things to worry about—like staying alive. That battle was later named "The Battle of Shit Hill." The sand hill was the public bathroom for the villages on both sides. As we dug in, some of the men also found out that the hill was used for quick, shallow burials. The smell of excrement on my face and the smell of rotten corpses made it difficult for me to enjoy my can of beefsteak with juices.

We got the word to prepare ourselves for air strikes, and indeed they began. First the helicopter gunships came in, pass after pass, using rockets and mini-guns, as we watched from our dug-in fighting positions. Following that, the jets came in extremely low, dropping 750-pound bombs. This presented a problem for us because we were too close to their target.

The shock from the bombs was unbelievable! Large pieces of metal and other debris were raining down on top of us. We were all attempting to hide under our helmets as pieces of bomb shrapnel landed all around us. I heard that down the line one of the men was killed by a huge dirt clod that came down on him. One bomb blast apparently penetrated one of the enemy's holes and blew him out like a cannon, straight up in the air about one hundred and fifty feet. Everybody started yelling, "Airborne!"

After the air strikes, we were still receiving some fire, but not nearly as much as before. The battle had pretty much ended for us, and we were all having dinner and watching the show. I felt very strange that I had just seen over three hundred and fifty human beings die right before my eyes and that I was a part of the massacre, not to mention the witnessing of so many of our guys being killed. This was an insane experience.

That night, we set up a couple of .50 caliber machine guns that would fire off and on all night long. Fifty-caliber machine guns had tremendous power and had a range of well over four miles. We watched the tracers streak through the village, bouncing around like wild golf balls and out the other side. Some of the rounds ricocheted straight up and disappeared into the clouds. It was like nothing could stop them.

It was cold in our positions that night. We had very little water, and nobody slept because there were still some enemy tracers (which were a different color from ours) being shot at us during the night. Also, we were afraid the enemy who were still alive might try to make a break for it in our direction. The enemy was offering us very little resistance because they had been blown to pieces.

The last air strike came later on that night when "Puff the Magic Dragon" (as we called the light gunships full of mini-guns) flew over. The aircraft would bank and let loose with thousands of rounds of mini-gun fire. Realizing that only one in three bullets was a tracer, it looked like solid fire breathing down on the village. After that, there was no more NVA firing at us.

The next morning we were able to leave our positions to go down to the back side of the sand hill for chow that they had flown in to us. There was a body near where each man was eating. The one next to me was named Pete; he had been a veteran jungle fighter for eight months. Another four and he would have been on his way home to his family.

I was so sad for the men who had died in the battle. We never knew how many of our own men died or the number of men that were wounded, because nobody cared enough to tell us. The three hundred and fifty NVA bothered me, too. I couldn't believe that I actually watched hundreds of people die right before my eyes and that I was part of the carnage. I wondered if the experience would leave me tainted for the rest of my life. I justified it thinking there was no other way; it was their offensive, and we were in defense mode. Before the battle, when they all knew they would die if they did not surrender, not one person waved the white flag. They all decided to die a very violent death rather than give up.

I racked my brain trying to understand what they must have believed in to make that sort of sacrifice. Were their minds full of lies and propaganda? Was it cultural loyalty, religious beliefs, or patriotism? Did they think their efforts might help in taking over other countries including America and the rest of the world? Were they all just ignorant and afraid to disobey, or dim-witted followers that would do anything they were ordered to do? I wondered what we would have done if the situation were reversed.

One NVA out of all of them ended up surviving. He was on a stretcher all bandaged up and acting friendly toward us. He was undoubtedly scared shitless. Someone came by and stuck a lit cigarette in his mouth, which he seemed to greatly appreciate. Wow! Somebody had offered a nice gesture. We should have offered those gestures on both sides before the battle. What a weird thought. I guessed he would be taken off and interrogated. I didn't know what would happen to that man.

Soon we would be heading to headquarters in the rear area for replacements and to reorganize. Our company commander was flown somewhere to a hospital, and we never knew whether he survived or not. I don't know how many casualties we had, but I am sure it was a significant number.

When we got back to the rear area, we would be staying in a specially designated area, away from headquarters and others. We would stay on concrete slabs that were about twenty feet wide and forty feet long. Each slab had shelter over the top to keep the rain off, but no walls. I hate to complain, but it was just bare concrete, no cots, no facilities, and a long walk to the showers. I think we must have felt as important as a bunch of cattle.

A truck showed up with hot chow and a ton of warm beer. We got clean clothes and just started drinking beer. It wasn't much of a party, but our friend from the rear who was once in our squad brought us a whole bunch of marijuana. We mostly sat quietly and got so intoxicated we passed out in place on the cement until morning—not having to stand guard duty.

Reorganization continued for about three days, and each day we did the same thing, or at least I think so. I was uncomfortable, depressed, and confused. I think morale would have been higher if the general had dropped by and said, "Nice job, men; sorry about your losses," or if we had been given some recognition or credit for what we had been through and accomplished. I think the higher-ups were basking in all the post-battle credit that would make our company and our battalion look good.

Also, we grunts had no idea that an offensive had taken place that involved all the major cities in Vietnam. We didn't know if the offensive was still going on somewhere else or what the extent of it was. We were isolated, not knowing what was going on with other units or, for that matter, what was going on in the rest of the Vietnam War. We rarely knew where we were or what the plan was. The only thing we knew was that the 173rd Airborne was a reactionary force for the central highlands.

I remember a few times receiving the *Stars and Stripes* military newspaper during re-supply, but the information presented seemed to be shallow and void of any real truth compared to what I was seeing and experiencing; it was something to which I could not relate. It just seemed to glorify the war.

I guess I could have requested newspapers from the states, but I think my loved ones were trying to protect me from what was being said so as not to discourage me. My family, bless their hearts, were very conservative people who I'm sure were upset with the way the war was portrayed by the media. I was a twenty-seven-year-old high school dropout and lacked the educational skills and tools to be able to analyze the whole thing.

I questioned what I had been taught to believe and was beginning to suffer from confusion and a bad feeling in my stomach. I had gotten myself into this situation and was going to try to make the best of it. I then formulated a goal that became stronger as time went on. If I survived and went home, I would immediately enroll in college. I wanted to learn about myself, and why I believed in what I did all my life that got me into this immoral mess. I wanted to pursue a massive self-analysis; but that would have to wait until my tour was over, and if I survived.

Our squad became extremely close, and we got to know each other so well that nothing about our character was hidden. Phony fronts did not hold up in the jungle or under fire. We were purely ourselves, and to survive we needed each other. Our main purpose was to fight for each other since we had no control over the war. We had gotten the word during a three-day stay in the rear that our platoon sergeant had lost a leg in a mine field trying to see the ladies in a village close by, or at least that was the scuttlebutt. I couldn't believe it because this sergeant was smart and a great guy.

# - 9 -

# CRAZY PARATROOPERS

Paratroopers were a different breed of soldier. They were more adventurous, wild, and crazy. They were physically stronger and had more endurance than the regular army guys. I guess that was why we were considered a reactionary force and dropped into areas highly populated by NVA. We were kept in the field for so long that when we were allowed some recreational time in town, we always got into trouble.

There was an instance in Dak To where someone threw a hand grenade close to a whorehouse, wounding several people, which put the whole place off-limits to us. I understand that there was a time when all villages in Vietnam were put off limits to the 173rd. I also understand that before I got there, a ranking officer actually designated a whole village of whorehouses just for us. He named this place "Dock Cock." This was perhaps the only nice thing officers ever did for us enlisted men. This may have been bullshit. It was short lived however, supposedly because of some general putting a stop to it.

One time, we were allowed to go into the air force base in Tuy Hoa. It was like walking into a stateside dream. The base had movies, cocktail lounges, hamburgers, snack bars, pool tables, and more. I don't understand why the air force had so much money and we didn't.

The first night we were allowed on the base, somebody slugged a high-ranking air force officer in the mouth, which rendered the air force base off-limits to us. Another time, some paratroopers got into a firefight in a bar on the base with South Korean troops, and it was off-limits again. Yet another time, about fifty of us were in a huge bar, having a wild time dancing with our shirts off, when a military policeman tried to exercise his authority to get things quieted down. The paratroopers picked him up over their heads, passed him around for about five minutes, and then threw him out the door on the other side of the room. After that we were not allowed to go to the air force base any longer.

For about the next five months, we ran into very little action. We worked the mountain areas of Tuy Hoa above the rice paddies and seemed to keep the NVA on the run. Occasionally we would walk into one of their large base camps while they were hightailing it out the other side. They would not fight us unless they were ready. It was spooky walking through a base camp that just moments before had accommodated a few hundred NVA. Clothing would be lying around and food would be cooking, but there was no sign of anybody. I guess we were just lucky, because other 173rd companies were seeing plenty of combat. We would run into a few enemy on the trail, but nothing big.

They would see us, and although they had weapons, they would run like hell. That was happening a lot. We would open up on them and maybe hit them, maybe not. The enemy we did kill would be decorated with our unit patch jammed into their foreheads and live grenades under their arms as booby traps. Some of the troops insisted on cutting off the ears of the enemy and wearing them around their necks. I could never get into doing that.

During this period, I was set on learning all I could about navigation in the jungle with map and compass and walking point. The position of point man was shared, and it seemed our squad's turn would come up often. Some men were very good at walking point and were used often, not necessarily taking turns. I was one of those men in my squad that was good at the job.

Walking point was nerve-racking, however, because the first man in front of the company was usually the first one to be hit if we ran into something. It was also nerve-racking because quite often the point man would scare up the animals as he walked along, which in turn would scare him into thinking momentarily that he had run into the enemy.

It was also the point-man's responsibility to uncover booby traps on the trail, which we had learned to identify. If there was loose dirt on a hard-packed trail, it could be a mine or a punji stick pit. Punji pits, which were covered by small branches and leaves, were filled with a bunch of sharpened sticks dipped in shit to cause infection. If a small branch hung across the trail, the point man would stop and carefully examine the branch to see if there was a wire on the other side that if moved would detonate a mortar round. We would mark these possible booby traps with toilet paper and simply walk around them.

Actually, most of the time, the company avoided walking on trails so we didn't have to worry that much about it. Our navigation was usually through the heavy, thick jungle. The point-man was also the person with a machete who would have to hack his way through to form a trail. Using a machete was extremely exhausting.

There was also a squad-sized unit called the "ranger element" that would travel a few hundred meters in front of the company. The purpose of this unit was to give the company time to maneuver in case they ran into something. They were kind of a sacrificial group. We navigated by French topographic maps and utilized mountains, rivers, and streams as points of reference. Our distance was calculated by how many meters we had traveled, provided to us by the pace counter.

It was important to know exactly where we were in case we had to immediately call in air strikes or artillery support. Our coordinates had to be very accurate so that we would not call these strikes in on ourselves, which tragically sometimes happened. Quite often at night, we could hear the distant rumbling of B-52 air strikes. They sounded devastating.

We found areas where strikes had occurred. I was not sure whether the bombs were 1000-or 2000-pounders. The blast from one of these bombs would clear a heavily foliaged area about seventy-five yards in diameter and leave a crater about thirty feet deep and thirty feet across. One of the guys found a spinal cord hanging on a branch along with other debris that looked like it had been surgically removed. In another one of these bomb sites somebody found an arm. The first sergeant played with it for a while, sticking it through his sleeve as if it were his own.

To me, napalm bombs couldn't compare to the large bombs. One time we were humping along a tree line next to an open area when an F-4 Phantom jet flew very low toward us. It dropped a napalm bomb that we watched tumble right over our heads and burst about a hundred feet on the other side of us. We could feel the heat. That was much too close. That was not the way I wanted to die. I don't know if it had been aimed at us by mistake or if the pilot made an error.

# - 10 -

# UNUSUAL ENCOUNTERS

O ur company held up for five days in a small valley. Usually we were on the move during the day, but for some reason the company's orders were to remain at this one location. Squads were sent off in a couple of directions about a half mile away to set up listening posts (LPs) in a place where the enemy was likely to approach. The LP would warn the company in case of an oncoming attack. It happened that our squad was serving as one of the LPs.

Our location was on the side of a hill where we would spend five days. We decided to make level beds of branches secured together with vines. We also constructed a table to eat on and crude chairs. In this particular area long vines hung down about fifty feet from tall trees. We would take a vine up the side of the hill and swing out into the jungle way above the ground on the low side. We were grateful not to be carrying heavy packs. We were supplied with a pallet containing food, water, mail, and clean clothes, which was lowered to us by helicopter.

We began taking it easy and enjoying ourselves; it was easy duty. By nightfall we had everything ready. Our fighting positions had been dug, and we had memorized the location of claymore mine detonators and grenades because the nights were pitch-black under the jungle canopy. You could not see your hand in front of your face.

That night we were awakened by distant noise. It sounded like many people coming toward us from about a hundred meters away, approaching fairly rapidly. I was scared to death as the noise got closer and closer. We started wondering who or what it was. I didn't see any flashlights, and I realized the enemy couldn't see any better than we could if there was zero visibility. How could anything see well enough to be moving along at the speed of a normal walk?

As it got closer, we knew it had to be a bunch of animals, but we had no idea what they were. We were ready for them to detonate the flares attached to our trip wires and were prepared for the whole area to be completely lit up. It sounded like maybe a hundred of them were coming right up to us, but amazingly they did not hit the trip wires on the flares, which would have given away our position to nearby NVA. We knew for sure at that point that they were animals because they had quick movements and couldn't weigh very much, because they were not breaking the twigs on the ground like a person would.

As we held our fire, we wondered what in the hell they could be. Suddenly they were on us and all around us. They were scurrying around eating our food and just messing around with us. They had absolutely no fear of being close to us, perhaps because they knew that we could not see them. They seemed to have perfect night vision. If I moved my arms quickly they would scatter temporarily and come right back. The man next to me let out a startled holler and said he had been poked by one of these things. Then they left as quickly as they came, without setting off one trip flare.

The next morning a lot of our food was missing, and everything in the camp had been disturbed, including personal items. They had also played around with our grenades, which could have easily exploded and killed us. We theorized that they had to be some sort of monkey or raccoon or something. We knew that they were capable of grasping, but, again, we were at a loss as to their identity. One man threw a rock where he thought one of them was and hit the animal. It hurt the beast, and he let out a horn-like honking noise. In the morning we all laughed about it and wrote letters back home about what we had experienced.

The next night, to our amazement, the animals came back, and we went through the same thing. This time, at least, we had the foresight not to straighten our grenade pins and to disconnect the trip flares just in case. The next morning after we had been visited for a second time, there was not a word said, just the hustle and bustle of men building various traps. We were so curious that, by God, we were going to catch one of these things to see what the hell it was.

One man made a snare trap by bending over just the right size tree with the steel cable used to deliver our rations. It was attached to a small notched-out tree about three inches from the ground, and close to the loop. The idea was that the animal would step in the loop and cause the notch attached to the tree to come loose and to spring up, suspending whatever it was in the self-tightening steel cable loop.

My trap was about three feet wide and three feet high with a sliding door attached to a stick. The stick was connected to another stick going down into the cage with a piece of food attached. When the animal went into the cage and took the food, the heavy gate would fall, trapping it inside. I learned to make it by watching my father catch opossums that were eating our chicken eggs.

Other men built similar traps. One of the traps consisted of a deep hole covered with branches. We worked almost the whole day, using our bayonets to cut the right sized material and securing everything together with strong vines. Before dusk we had completed the task, and we waited with great anticipation for their return. Around midnight we heard them coming again, and we heard traps around us being sprung, as we had planned.

The next morning two traps had been sprung, but we had not captured one animal. The side of my trap had been either broken or gnawed away, as were the others. The steel cable on the snarl trap was actually broken in two, or gnawed in half. That was pretty amazing because that cable was so strong you could have towed a car with it. The next night, to our disappointment, they did not show up again. In the morning, we were called back to the company and moved out. I found out in college several years later that those animals must have been rock apes, which were about two and a half feet tall.

One noise common to us in the central highlands was the chanting of the famous "Fuck you" lizard. I know this sounds crazy, but there was, and maybe still is, a lizard in some parts of Vietnam that would yell, "Fuck you," all night long. It was a green lizard, a foot and a half long, and it was very mean. It first sounded like a series of winding-up clicking noises followed by a loud repetition of, "Fuck you, fuck you, fuck you," that got weaker and weaker until it stopped. The noise it made sounded exactly like somebody screaming in a high-pitched voice. If you poked at this lizard with a stick, it would snap it in half with its strong jaws. Interestingly, its disposition matched its colorful vocabulary as it let us know verbally we weren't welcome.

I had heard about the lizard from some guys in the squad, but I thought it was a prank and that they were testing me to see how stupid I was. At first, I did not believe it. After I heard the lizards, I couldn't help wondering if they would sell big in Hollywood or somewhere as a novelty pet. How cool it would have been for people to have a lizard in their apartment that yelled, "Fuck you," every night. Nobody except the people way out in the jungle knew what it sounded like or believed it existed. We used to talk about how rich we could become by importing these animals when we got home, but just getting home was our main focus and all we wanted to think about.

One morning we were taking in the trip flares and claymores from an uneventful ambush at a French-made canal when we heard a loud splash. We all hit the ground ready to fire as a mountain lion bounded by so closely we could have reached out and touched it. The lion was coming from the direction of the rice paddies and was heading back into the jungle. It was beautiful with rippling muscles, great power, and speed. I could only imagine that he was eating the people in the rice paddies because I didn't think there was wild game out there. Rice paddies took up most of the Tuy Hoa Valley with occasional small, scattered islands where the people lived who worked the fields.

# - 11 -

## ATROCITIES

We would hear stories, some about our own company, from the support unit people about atrocities being committed by the infantrymen. It has been my experience that all of these stories were little more than bullshit. Only twenty percent of the soldiers in 173rd did the actual fighting. The other eighty percent were support people—cooks, ammunition suppliers, carriers, communications, and so forth.

The stories of atrocities and exaggerations seemed to come from these support people. Maybe it was because of guilt, or maybe feelings of inadequacy or spite at not having been in the actual fighting. It was embarrassing, I suppose, for a person in the rear area to return home to friends and family and have to explain that they were a clerk typist or something. I wished they didn't feel that way, as the support people were critical to the whole operation.

I don't remember ever witnessing anybody shooting women and children or innocent people or torturing prisoners. This could have been happening in other units like the Lieutenant Calley incident at My Lai, which everybody read about in the papers, where women and children were shot. It could have been that these were inexperienced men who were scared and a little trigger-happy because of it. There is quite a range of fear in a combat zone and because of it they may have overreacted. Our unit was in so much combat that we had no trouble at all separating the enemy from the innocent villagers we occasionally ran across.

In some villages our medic was sent in to try to treat the people for infections and other medical problems. I used to always volunteer to go with Doc to provide for his security because I enjoyed playing with the children and passing out candy, what little candy we had. Doc would do the best he could, given the limited supplies he had. The people who lived in these remote villages would get skin infections from all the bacteria. The infections would look like red ping-pong balls growing on their skin. I guess their immune systems, having evolved over thousands of years, protected them by localizing infections that would not spread (hence the red balls on their skin).

Doc would hand out some soap to these people, which he said was a great way to prevent infections. They had no medical care whatsoever except for those practices and different herbs that were handed down through their culture and traditions. I remember seeing one lady in a hut who was dying after being gored by a water buffalo. There was nothing anyone could do because the army was not about to fly a civilian to a hospital. I think it was just too risky for the American pilots, and of course they were too busy taking care of American soldiers.

We saw a boy about seven or eight years old who had severely cut his foot across the arch. The wound had healed, but for the rest of his life the front part of his foot dangled and flopped as he walked. Surgery would have taken care of that back in the states, but not for this kid, not in this place. Doc was a hard-core medic who was never gentle with the troops, but he was very gentle with the children and adult villagers.

# - 12 -

# STANDARDS

O ur packs were heavy with all the weaponry, food, and ammunition, especially after re-supply. To get off the ground we had to roll over on our stomachs, rise to our hands and knees, and with the help of a nearby tree or friend be pulled to our feet. Our ammunition and weaponry were carried on separate harnesses, and our pack was carried over that by just two shoulder straps. There was no waist belt to support the weight, just our shoulders.

If we made contact with the enemy we could quickly throw our packs off, keeping our ammo harnesses on and be ready to fight. We carried five hundred M16 rounds in pre-loaded magazines. We carried at least two smoke grenades to let air strike pilots know where we were, as the smoke would drift up through the jungle canopy. We also carried an 81mm mortar round on the top of our packs, which we could pass over to the mortar tube if needed. Some of us carried one Willy Peter (white phosphorus) grenade.

One person in each squad carried a grenade launcher, and one person from the weapons platoon carried the M60 machine gun over his shoulder. I only remember one white man who ever carried a machine gun. The rest of the machine gun carriers were black. Machine gunners had a short lifespan, and I assume this was because they were more of a target. They were elevated higher than riflemen because of the tripod that held up the front of the gun. Most people in the squad would carry the machine gunner's ammo, which consisted of two hundred round belts each. That would also be passed to the machine gunner if we made contact with the enemy.

We carried all of this weight for miles every day through streams, up and down hills, and through thick jungles. I think back on it and wonder how we could have possibly endured that punishment. We were like animals as we marched along. We had a saying in our company that if you were exhausted and could not possibly go any farther, you would take out the "drive-on rag," wipe the sweat out of your eyes and just keep putting one foot in front of the other. That drive-on rag philosophy came in handy after the war when I ran into difficult situations.

C-Rations and freeze-dried food were very valuable stuff. It was like currency that we often traded with each other. Each type of food had value, some expensive and some with very little value. The most popular and consequently the most expensive foods were canned peaches and canned pound cake. Also of value were cigarettes. Non-smokers would often trade them with the other soldiers for different foods that they really liked. The least valued food on the list was canned ham and lima beans, which we called "ham and mother-fuckers." Most everyone hated those damn things. However, there was one man from Mississippi who loved them, and during re-supply there was a big rush over to him to trade our ham and mother-fuckers for something more tasty like peanut butter, canned beefsteak with juices, or canned fruitcake. We believed that if we provided the enemy with lots of ham and mother-fuckers, we could win the war.

We were so tired of the food that we invented ingenious ways of preparing it and mixing it. One time as a joke, some insensitive friends from the states sent our squad a box of dog biscuits. The joke was on the sender however, because we all ate them and enjoyed them immensely. Any seasoning sent from loved ones was solid gold. Once in a while, we would share with each other our fantasies of what we would eat when we got back to the states. We talked about ice cream, juicy hamburgers, ribs, potato salad, pie, fresh fruit, fresh bread, and so forth. These fantasies, including those about women, would give us something to try to stay alive for. We set goals of heavenly things to achieve and enjoy if we made it home.

The makeup of the squads was usually permanent. The nine-man squad was your family. Trying to protect each other in battle became our main focus and reason to fight. The whole company consisted of a fragmented sum total of squads, functioning sometimes as part of the company, but, for the most part, functioning independently. For instance, our squad didn't really know what other squads were doing. Our squad was our reality, our home, our world. A squad was a tight, very cohesive group. A platoon (about thirty men) was a less cohesive group, and a company of four other platoons wouldn't know each other very well at all.

We had to remain separated from each other by about three meters to avoid taking too many casualties. Sometimes in our squad, if one of us was sick, he was allowed to sleep through the night without having to stand guard position. Also, when somebody was sick, we usually divided up his weight and carried it for him. We shared intimate stories and had moments of laughter. If you survived a year, that bond between soldiers would last a lifetime.

We were just a few feet from each other day and night. We smelled each other's bad smells constantly. There is a limit as to how badly one can smell, unless we cut loose down our pant legs with diarrhea. We just all kind of got used to it. Nobody smelled the same. Each of us had our own unique body odor, and it sort of became part of our identity. At night when we couldn't see our hands in front of our faces, we knew the identity and location of fellow squad members by smell. Although we didn't express it verbally back in those days, we loved each other.

The enemy also had an odor but their smell was smoky, like a bacon smell. They had to be secretive with their fires and would huddle close. If we smelled that odor, we knew we were close. And likewise, if they smelled our rotten stench, they knew we were close as well. Their fires were built on the sides of hills with a trench that ran up a hundred feet or so. The trench or chimney would be covered with branches and leaves so the smoke would be dispersed evenly through the branches and would be harder to notice from the air.

Probably one of the most frightening things we had to do on a regular basis was setting up a squad-sized ambush site every third night. It was much safer staying with our company, which provided safety in numbers. The company rarely stayed in the same place more than one night. Squads were sent out to set up ambushes in places where we could most likely catch the enemy marching along at night. Of course there had to be moonlight and at least a sparse area so we could see what we were doing.

The enemy mostly moved at night and traveled in small numbers of six to ten. The real danger, however, would be killing the people who walked through the kill zone and then realizing there were a hundred or more NVA coming down the trail who, when attacked, would immediately encircle the small ambush unit and snuff them out. One never knew exactly how many enemy they would be encountering. I heard from squads that, more than once, large numbers of enemy were allowed to walk through their kill zone.

The ambush had to be set up where the trail curved so you could see what was coming in both directions. It had to be set up behind bushes so that while we were close to the trail we could not be seen.

One night it was raining very hard, and we could not smell each other. The visibility was poor, and I allowed the enemy to walk through just about six feet from us. I was on guard at the time, and as I watched them go by through the bush in front of me, my heart was in my throat. I was afraid the enemy could hear it beating. I think others in the squad may have felt the same on occasion.

I remember thinking that if we were not detected, why risk losing our lives? This was at a time during my tour when we started questioning more and more why we were in Vietnam and if it was worth dying for. If we were fighting for our country, it would have been different, but we were not, and I didn't think fighting for South Vietnam was worth dying for. The indigenous people were ignorant and just wanted to work their rice fields and survive.

We talked with each other on a regular basis about why we were there and why all this death was taking place. We concluded that the war was crazy, and we were trapped in it and had no place to go. It is not mentioned in our history books that American soldiers would ever question their involvement in a war. What we were talking about could have been interpreted back in the States as cowardice, or maybe even treason. What we didn't know at the time was that people back home were starting to seriously protest the war.

We didn't know that Secretary of State Robert McNamara would later in his book admit that there was no plan to win that war and that we couldn't, in fact, win that war.

Our squad leader finished his time in Vietnam and was going home, but not without being wounded by shrapnel when the NVA walked mortar rounds right over the company during a major battle in Dak To before I went into the field. He was a nice man and very bright. He taught me how to call in artillery and air strikes using the topographic map. I learned as much as I possibly could from him, thinking that someday I could become a sergeant and squad leader myself.

What I didn't like about this man was that he followed orders to the letter. If he was ordered to take his squad one hundred meters, he would go exactly one hundred meters no matter how dangerous it was to do so. The reason I wanted to become a squad leader was so I could make decisions for the squad, and in dangerous situations I could alter my orders, unknown to the platoon sergeant, thus increasing the probability of my men and me surviving the war and going home still possessing a pulse.

I was promoted to sergeant and took over the squad. Whether there was an ambush or some other contact with the enemy, the squad leader had to keep a cool head. I practiced staying calm every day and in every situation we encountered. I needed to think clearly and function well even though I was scared to death. After a while I developed this strange sense. Over time I was able to cultivate the skill of accurately discerning the degree of danger we were in and acting accordingly. It was easy for new men to become so scared that they were unable to function and to make dangerous mistakes like sometimes blasting away at the bushes with their weapon unnecessarily.

Another frightening operation was called a heliborne assault. I don't remember exactly how many of these assaults I made (maybe in the twenties) but it was enough to earn the Air Medal. These assaults took place in areas where Intelligence determined there was a large concentration of the enemy.

Before we were flown in, artillery would prep the area. Immediately after the artillery would cease fire, many helicopters, carrying six grunts each, would fly in and hover a few feet off the ground while we jumped off and formed a perimeter. I'd heard that a few times door gunners on a chopper would accidentally kill somebody jumping off who got in the line of fire.

As we settled down, the helicopter door gunners would be blasting away, hopefully keeping the enemy at bay while we jumped off. The grunts would sit in the doorway three on each side. It was always my rotten luck that the ground would not be level on my side. The guys on the other side could just step off a foot or so, but on my side, I had a three to six foot jump to the ground. With all the weight we were carrying, the danger of broken legs and knee injuries was high.

We learned to scoot off the helicopter like we were going to land on our stomachs and do a little twist, landing on our backs on top of our packs to cushion the fall. I always worried while doing this because we attached grenades to our webbing and carried mortar rounds on top of our packs.

As we were approaching the landing zone, grass fires would be burning, caused by the artillery, and it always looked like the landing zone was "hot," but most of the time, thank God, it was not. Helicopter assaults were our main form of transportation for going deep into enemy territory, somehow verified by Army Intelligence.

# - 13 -

# BIZARRE BODY COUNT

Body count was extremely important to the 173rd Airborne Brigade, and probably to every other unit in Vietnam. Numbers were important, and I knew that the numbers of dead enemy were no exception. I think counting bodies was important because it was a way to evaluate how well our company was doing compared to other units. The practice was a measure of our success. I always suspected that companies in our unit competed against each other for body count. Moreover, I think battalions in our unit competed against each other as well.

Counting bodies was a sick way, in my opinion, for officers in charge to gain military prestige and status and to prove their worth. I believe officers with high body counts from the men in their command would make them look good and could be more easily promoted to a higher rank. I also think that, in order to advance their careers, they needed to acquire medals for valor, which they achieved rather easily by writing each other up. Officers never walked point, they never physically led an assault, and they never went out to spend the night on ambush. They certainly never had to personally dig up enemy graves for a body count. I am sure, however, that they received all of the recognition.

Enlisted men did not write each other up for medals. It was the responsibility of officers to do this for them. I know because I tried doing it on two occasions, but I think they were trashed when they got to the rear area, because I never heard back. I believe the reason enlisted men received very few medals and were not given full recognition was because they were thought of as a bunch of stupid grunts who were not very important anyway—just pawns in a chess game.

During our marches we would often run across large and small graves where the enemy had buried their dead. We were always ordered to dig up those graves and count the bodies so our company could take credit. One grave had been dug up by other units and buried again so many times the arms and legs had become detached, making it difficult to get an accurate count. That was probably the most disgusting job we had to do. I can't tell you how badly the bodies smelled.

It seems crazy to me that graves would be dug up over and over again. It didn't matter if other units had dug them up. It didn't matter because the more they were dug up and counted, the higher the count. Of course officers never had to do this work. Their job was merely to record the numbers. This body count business just added to the grand insanity. I remember years after I got home, General Westmoreland, who was in charge of the war, got caught lying about the body count. It was somebody from *60 Minutes* who exposed him. This was one of the major scandals of the war.

Units in Vietnam uncovered underground hospitals. They found empty penicillin bottles and other paraphernalia from the states. The enemy spent a lot of time underground while we marched over them trying to find them. We once found a training area above the ground that had grenades made out of wood and simulated barbed wire made out of vines.

Their weapon, the AK-47, was superior to our M16. During the time I was over there, our M16s only held a 20-round clip as compared to the enemy's 30-round clips. On top of that, our 20-round clips would really only hold eighteen rounds because any more than that would cause a malfunction, which put us at a real disadvantage. The NVA were extremely disciplined compared to us American grunts. They could sit on their haunches for long periods, never making a sound. We would walk along making clanking noises and rustling through bushes.

If it weren't for air strikes, artillery, and gunships, we could not have won our battles, because the enemy was superior to us in many ways.

# - 14 -

# DRUGS IN THE FIELD

D rugs, at least in our company, were not used unless we were in the rear or pulling security duty around a fire-support base on a mountaintop. A fire-support base with 105mm howitzers was fairly secure, for the most part, although they were occasionally overrun.

Our drug of choice was marijuana. I don't know if we had any other connection for other drugs. Men coming into the company would usually bring some to share with others, but the situation had to be safe enough, so our use of drugs was pretty rare. We had to be hyper-alert and ready to fight twenty-four hours a day, and drug use would have been pretty damn reckless and irresponsible. Drugs were dangerous not only to ourselves but to the people around us.

There was a time when I first came to Vietnam that our unit was at a large base camp at Hon Kai. I think we were sharing that big base camp with another army unit called the 1st Cavalry. There was a large wire cage of sorts in the middle of the base where people partied at night. Somebody had set up a stereo and had all the latest recordings from the sixties. It was very much out of the ordinary. We sat in a circle around the fence, listened to music, and passed a pipe around that contained opium. I got so high that I could swear I was levitating right off the ground. I had to reach back and feel the ground to make sure gravity was still working.

The amazing thing about this party place was that certainly the command knew about it. I didn't know the people in the circle. I just stumbled onto it and invited myself in. I believe it was the 1st Cavalry who allowed this to happen and just turned a blind eye. I know that the l73rd would not have allowed such a luxury to exist.

# - 15 -

# BIG MISTAKE

One morning our company was moving along when the point element ran into a huge base camp. About fifty NVA who did not know we were there were swimming and taking baths in a river about thirty feet wide. There was a dirt bank that the point element was peeking over, undetected. Their weapons were leaning against trees. Because of the noise of the flowing water, they did not hear us and were totally unaware of our presence.

We moved up and lined the riverbank. We could hear them talking and having a great time. They were about twenty-five feet away from the point element. If there were ever a more perfect time to make an assault, this was it.

Our company commander was new and careful, and I think he was scared. He decided to pull back and set up ambushes on what he thought were the escape routes. He then called in air strikes, thinking that the enemy would come running out of there and that we would kill them as they ran out. The company commander was surprised when they all ran out in a different direction.

We wounded one of them. He was the only one that came our way. The wounded man was questioned by our interpreter but wasn't able to speak due to his wounds. Our medic was ordered by the company commander to shoot him as he lay on the ground writhing in pain. The M16 was placed to the man's head as we all stood around watching, and the trigger was pulled.

The M16 has a tremendous velocity, and the man's head exploded. Brains flew all over us. People reacted in a joking manner, complaining, "Thanks a lot, Doc," as they wiped the brains, hair, and bone fragments off of them. The man's head was gone all except for his face, which looked like a thin mask people might wear on Halloween.

Word was passed down the next morning from the company commander's radio operator (one of our men) that he had been chewed out seriously from headquarters because he didn't make the assault. He was told, according to the radio operator, that his job was to kill the enemy, not to move back.

When I heard that I got a sick feeling in my stomach. I knew that no matter what we ran into, how big or how dangerous it was, he would assault. I'm sure the company commander did the right thing with the safety of our troops in mind, being new and conscientious, but the big brass at headquarters was pissed off because they did not get their body count.

# - 16 -

## VILLAGE IDIOT

When our lieutenant had been killed by a booby trap, we got a new officer. He was black, and he treated us well. He didn't seem to care much about what the other officers felt; he just wanted to survive and go home. I started thinking that as a black man he must have felt discrimination from the other officers because he was pretty much a loner. After all, this was the sixties, and there was all that Southern hatred for blacks, which had to spill over into the military at least a bit, although I couldn't see it. The civil rights movement was happening back in the States. I'm certain that he was the one who wrote me up for the Bronze Star during the Tet.

Officers are only required to spend six months in the field, and his time was up, so he was headed for the rear to spend the rest of his tour. We were happy for him. His replacement, our new lieutenant, was a man who surprisingly was not good at all at reading a map. I knew this because he would ask me about the best way to go. It was evident that he didn't know much about jungle warfare.

He was new, so I guess that was to be expected. Someone had said that his father was a high ranking general in the military and that he had been passed along through officers' school. I didn't know if that was true or not, but what worried me the most was that he would be required to call in air strikes and artillery if our platoon were ever in real trouble. We were afraid if that happened, he was going to get us all killed.

I suppose we should have shown him compassion and tried to help him in some way and maybe even trusted him as our officer, but this was serious life and death stuff, and it was just a matter of time before he possibly got us killed by making some stupid mistake. I had heard that during Vietnam "fragging," the killing of a fellow soldier with a grenade, was sometimes practiced, but no one in our company that I knew had ever killed one of our own.

As time went on, I became more worried, because he didn't seem to be learning, so I finally decided to have a talk with him about our fears. I met to quietly talk with him one night at our harbor site. I explained our fears to him, and I told him not to dare try to call in air strikes. I said it in the most positive way I could. He knew that we knew he wasn't capable, and his response to me was a quiet, "Okay, Sergeant." He knew he was not able to do the job, and I suspect the company commander and other officers knew it as well.

Anyway, for the first time I felt like I had some control over a little piece of the madness and that maybe I had prevented something terrible from happening. As I relieved myself on a bush, a smile came over my face. For the first time, I felt a tinge of liberation.

Our company would be leaving our area of operation (AO), which was good because an enemy we had killed a few days earlier was beginning to smell very bad. The stench of a rotting corpse can be detected a mile away. I remember once we were marching past an enemy soldier we had killed two days earlier, and the corpse was beginning to smell. The company had stopped just long enough to grab some lunch. One man sat right next to the body and opened up a can of meat and began to chow down. I guess it was an opportunity for him to prove he was "hard-core" when in reality I'm sure he wanted to vomit.

# - 17 -

# THE SQUAD

I n my squad there was no hierarchy of duties. You might say it was nonmilitary in nature. As a sergeant I really didn't give orders in the military sense. Rather, I asked people to do things. Many decisions were discussed and reached by consensus. We were rather democratic, which was not the military way. Our new platoon sergeant used to give me a hard time about the way I treated the squad. I used to remind him that I would run my squad the way I wanted.

There was a new man in the squad who was just eighteen and could have used some combat experience for the job ahead. Even though he was scared to death, having heard about the company's combat history, he was conscientious, careful, and eager to learn. He stayed fairly close to me most of the time as we did our daily patrols. I took care of him because he was new, and we all watched out for him.

One day, about five days before he died, he complained of having something in his eye. I flushed it with water a few times, and I looked into it several times that day but couldn't see anything. He declined to bother the medic about it. I knew very little about his family, but he seemed like a good kid. To this day, I think about looking closely and marveling at the complexity of the living eye that soon would not see.

Another man, Jim, was an in-depth thinker, an adventure lover, an intellectual, and a bookworm. He often talked about anthropology, which he was studying in college before he got drafted. He was more of an introvert than the others.

Yet another man called "Dee" (short for Stanley De Ruggerrio) was from New York. He was a wiry, physically strong Italian with penetrating eyes. He fit the stereotype of a gangster. He looked like one, talked like one, however, it was not his nature.

He carried the heaviest backpack in the whole company. He was a walking kitchen and carried spices, herbs, and some other things on top of his regular C-Rations. People would come to him and ask for a little garlic or oregano, and he was happy to share.

He was a veteran jungle fighter before I arrived in the company and had fought in the Battle of Hill 875. He was tough, ballsy, and really knew his stuff. He was a good friend and always loyal. Later we would both end up saving each other's lives.

# - 18 -

# THE AMBUSH

O ur company was notified that we would be going to a place about seventy-five miles north of Saigon, and I think it was about a hundred and fifty miles from where we were operating with the rest of the 173rd Airborne Brigade. Our mission was to locate and destroy a battalion of NVA who were kicking ass on the South Vietnamese troops in the area.

Later we learned we would be the only U.S. forces in the area. We would be way out of range of any artillery support, and it would take at least an hour to receive air support if we got into trouble. It would also take twenty-four hours for any American troops to be able to come to our rescue; we would be isolated.

It is my opinion that our company was being punished for the time that we pulled back from the large base camp that we should have assaulted. Our company was going to be placed in a position of real disadvantage. It would be ninety of us against over three hundred of them. I felt like we were being sacrificed, pure and simple. It was obvious to all of us that the enemy would not hesitate to fight us under these conditions. Of course we were just getting the information handed down to us, and I didn't know for sure how much of it was true. For the first time, everybody seemed to be communicating, probably because what we were going into was a very dangerous situation.

This mission just reinforced my beliefs that the high command had no regard for our lives. They just wanted to play the big game and get their body count. This was indeed a sickening feeling, knowing that none of us could do a damn thing about it, and most of us having known for a long time that the war wasn't worth the sacrifice of our lives. I'm sure even the company commander realized what was going on and that there was nothing he could do about it either. In my opinion, he was under pressure to make good after his last blunder.

We were being led into death like lambs to the slaughter. But then, this was war, and that was what we were supposed to do, regardless of how reckless it was. Later in life I talked to a retired Green Beret, who served three tours in Vietnam, who told me that sending a small company that far away into isolation without adequate support was unheard of.

Body count was important, the enemy body count that is, not ours. Through it all, the high command would be in the rear sitting on their asses in safety and comfort. The focus would be them. I think they wanted their command, whoever they were, to think of them as tough, elite, daring, and eager to carry out dangerous battles.

I thought what we were about to do was unnecessary; for that matter, the whole damn war was unnecessary. By the end of the Vietnam War, we were to lose over sixty thousand American soldiers. God knows how many soldiers, survivors, and families on both sides would suffer immeasurable grief. In time, America would just quit and go home. The big game of death would be over, and it would be time to start planning for the next big game, because war was the American way.

Eventually, because of the ongoing outcry from people opposed to the war, the politicians in Washington were losing their support and were beginning to get nervous. So like good politicians, and because of pressure from the growing anti-war movement, they started changing color and began to oppose the war themselves, causing it to come to an end. The Vietnam War would cause a major cultural and social revolution in this country, which I will talk about later.

When we arrived in at this place, the enemy had been ambushing traffic on Highway 1, which amounted to a simple dirt road but was a major supply line from South to North Vietnam. For the first few days we would be rushed to these areas to patrol both sides of the highway but find nothing. We were then operating in a huge tea-growing area, a plantation of perhaps thousands of acres. This plantation was worked by a Frenchman, who claimed to be a neutral. I figured he would not be allowed to operate and his business would not be allowed to exist if he didn't pay plenty of taxes to the NVA, but he denied this. The interpreter who talked to the Frenchman told us that the tea was harvested twice a year and that it would bring thousands of dollars per acre.

We were then sent across the river into the thick jungle on the other side of the highway to continue our search. It was during the monsoon, and the leeches were profuse. We were spending a lot of our time removing leeches from each other with insect repellent. After a couple of days of searching, we started to find signs in the form of footprints and small trails, and we knew we were getting close.

The next day the company was following a large trail when an AK-47 opened up on our rear. Word was passed along on the radio that the last man in our company had been hit. We theorized that they let us pass by to see how many we were and then opened fire on the last man. One platoon stayed back to cut a hole in the canopy to wait for a helicopter evacuation of the wounded man.

Both our platoon and the other one were patrolling side by side about a hundred yards apart on a sweep. We got to a small, open rice paddy and started moving across in the water toward the thick jungle on the other side. We were almost across when from a small island four or five AK-47s opened up to our front, wounding three more men. We immediately returned the fire and rushed their location, but they were gone.

This was beginning to get spooky, as they appeared to be playing with us. Squads were sent out to form a perimeter so we could take care of the wounded and wait for the dust off to arrive. Two of the men were shot up pretty badly. One man had his penis shot off and a bullet wound through his leg. I told the man, "You're going home, and you will never have to hump these boonies again." He replied, "Yeah, Sergeant Roberts, but this is a hell of a way to be going home."

After the wounded were flown out, we joined up with the rest of the company, moved forward again, and set up a harbor sight for the night. We also set up an ambush on the small island from where we had been attacked. That night was uneventful.

The next day we ran across a small base camp and went in with guns blazing, but nobody was there. We set up a perimeter in the small NVA base camp, hoping they would come back. Squad-size patrols were sent out in all directions, which I wasn't too happy about. I only went about half the distance that I was supposed to go. The platoon lieutenant came with us and didn't realize what I had done. I didn't like the idea of a squad-size patrol in an area infested with NVA.

We came up with nothing more that day. The whole company then moved back about eight hundred meters to set up a harbor site for the night. Then the company commander decided to send our platoon back to that small base camp just before dark to set up an ambush, thinking the enemy would return that night. During that night, nobody slept a wink. We used enemy holes for our fighting positions and set up a perimeter. Being scared shitless was becoming a way of life. It wasn't just me. Everybody was scared out of their minds. You could see it in their eyes.

Fortunately, that night was also uneventful. For a short time we had been working with a Vietnamese scout team consisting of a South Vietnamese lieutenant and a few men under him. We had never done that before. I was impressed with the lieutenant, who seemed to know what he was doing; but I was not so impressed with a few of the men under him. Of course I didn't know for sure how well they would do under fire, nor did I trust them.

The next day we saw more fresh trails and more signs of the enemy. Our platoon was second to the point. The point platoon started catching glimpses of the enemy just ahead of them. The platoon was hearing Vietnamese voices as we continued to move forward, following them. We all knew that this was a day we were going to run into something major. They were obviously leading us into their web, and everybody knew it.

As we moved along, we made our final personal preparations for the battle ahead. I had a hollow feeling in my stomach and felt that this was probably my last day of life. In my prayers, I thought of home and my loved ones and what a mess I had made of my life. I'm sure everyone was thinking the same thing, at least about their families and loved ones.

Just ahead I heard our M60 machine gun open up with a long burst, and several M16s started crackling. The enemy rounds were coming from the front as we moved in fast to crush their fire to gain fire superiority. The rounds were coming in at us just over our heads as we were moving up a slope. I looked up to observe the bullets moving through the leaves. I saw a line of leaves thirty to forty feet long all move at the same time, which gave me the realization of how fast the bullets were traveling. The incoming fire began to get worse but was only from the front as we moved forward.

All of a sudden, the enemy was at our right flank with three American-made grenade launchers starting to fire at us. The M79 grenade launcher had a sound that we were all familiar with. We knew exactly what it was. Grenades were exploding all around us along with AK-47 fire. Our stupid lieutenant thought that because these were American weapons, the platoon on the other side must be firing at us accidentally. He started yelling, "Stop firing!" and told us at the same time to hold our fire. He was yelling, "Hey, it's us! Don't shoot!" The rounds kept coming in and no one was returning the fire. The enemy was attacking us with our own weapons. I heard later that a Special Forces camp not too far away had been overrun and our weapons had been taken.

We were starting to get chopped up. I gave the order for my squad to start firing, and we opened up. Others followed suit, and the battle was on. The fire toward us became intense, and we were throwing a lot back. I estimated that the enemy was fifteen to thirty feet away, but we could not see them in the underbrush. I knew the M79 grenade launchers were very close, because they needed more distance for the grenade to arm itself after being fired and many rounds went past us without exploding.

If that wasn't bad enough, the left flank opened up on us with the same intensity of fire. All you could hear was a deafening roar. At that point, we all became horrified, realizing that we had been led right into a horseshoe ambush. Just a month or two earlier we had heard that a whole company had been wiped out in one of these ambushes.

It was total bedlam, and a lot of people were screaming for the medic. The new guy in the squad just ten feet away was yelling for help. Two of us crawled over to him. A bullet had gone through his upper arm, into his chest, and out the other side. In his agony, he stared into my face with a look that said, "God, somebody please help me." Doc was way too busy working on other men, so we had to try to stop the bleeding ourselves. We lifted up his arm and saw that the hole in his chest was emitting blood like a faucet. The man was dying quickly, and there was nothing we could do for him. We crawled back to our positions a few feet away and continued to lay down fire. The fire was unbelievable. The rounds were tearing trees apart and hitting the ground all around us.

The way a horseshoe ambush works is that soldiers are drawn in from fire in front. They go charging in full force to gain fire superiority. Then the right and the left flanks start pouring in fire, the rear closes, and you are trapped. The enemy begins to run through you, breaking up everybody into small groups. Disoriented and unable to effectively defend themselves, the enemy begins to snuff out individual groups until everyone is killed. I had heard of this happening before, and now it was happening to our company.

To our advantage, one platoon had stayed back to prepare an evacuation point for the wounded, and the other platoon had briefly retreated because of the heavy fire, leaving our platoon alone. Because of this they were never able to surround us completely. A couple did run through us firing and screaming in an effort to try to break us up into small groups. The enemy failed to accomplish this because everybody started yelling to move toward the middle to form one perimeter where we could more effectively provide a defense and possibly survive. We were able to achieve this and were huddled closely together in a circle to put out maximum fire.

The platoon that had retreated broke back in to help us. Despite being greatly outnumbered, with most of us wounded and many dead, we were effectively holding them off. The South Vietnamese scout unit lieutenant had apparently called in air strikes, and they were about to arrive. The Vietnamese officer had tried to call in air strikes, but he had been killed.

Somehow the captain of our unit had come to the front and had been shot. I think he jumped into what he thought was a shallow hole for cover, but the hole turned out to be a nine-foot deep well with a small amount of water at the bottom. He could not get out to command the company, and he had no way of communicating with anyone; he had no radio and couldn't be heard over the roar of the battle. He was stuck but out of the way of incoming fire unless the enemy tossed a grenade in there, which didn't happen. The fire was too intense to rescue him at that time.

When we all moved to the middle to try to save ourselves, the dead and the wounded were left about fifteen feet outside our small perimeter. Two men in my squad decided to go back out for the wounded. One of the men dragged back a wounded man, but he died.

The other man found a badly-wounded man but could not drag him back because numerous NVA were crawling in toward him blasting their automatic weapons, trying to penetrate our perimeter. The wounded man happened to be next to a termite mound about three feet high. DeRuggerio (Dee), using the mound as cover, killed every one of the enemy as they moved forward. Incoming rounds were pulverizing the mound and the termites were eating him alive. Despite this and the fact that he had taken shrapnel wounds in the hip, Dee continued to hold them off, protecting the wounded man, who later, despite his multiple wounds, survived. His actions also saved my life, keeping those NVA from getting to me.

Years later, the wounded man told the story of being badly wounded and unable to move. He heard many NVA talking and crawling toward him. He was going to shoot himself rather than be captured and tortured to death, but suddenly someone was kneeling over him, protecting him and firing like crazy. He never knew who had saved him until twenty years later; it was Dee.

Our platoon was being hacked to pieces. The captain could not get out of the hole, and the Vietnamese lieutenant who was going to call in air strikes was dead. Our lieutenant who was not capable of calling them in had remembered our talk, I guess, and was not attempting to do so, thank God. I had been studying how to call in air strikes for months just in case I ever had to and I realized the time was at hand.

I crawled up to the dead lieutenant who had the radio and realized that it was up to me—that it was the only way we could possibly survive. The lieutenant was lying face down. The brains that had been blown out of his head were lying on his back. I grabbed the radio and scooted back because the rounds were moving the grass a couple of inches from my face.

I stopped and played dead for a few moments while I very slowly got a fix on where that particular fire was coming from. I could barely see an NVA in the crotch of a tree about ten feet off the ground and about forty feet away. I could barely make him out through an opening in the trees. I turned quickly and fired a burst at him and saw him fall.

I picked up the radio and became paralyzed with fear. I just knew I was going to die. I thought about killing myself rather than being captured. I entered into a total panic, unable to think or move.

I had joined a church before I had left for Nam, and I had learned to pray. That's exactly what I did. I don't remember my prayer, but all of a sudden a strange calmness fell over me. My mind became clear, and I was able to have a laser-like concentration on what I was about to do.

I made contact with a chopper gunship with mini-guns that had arrived on the scene. I directed the pilot to come in from east to west because he had to be very close—within a few feet of being on top of us. On the radio the pilot told me that he would start firing and for me to holler, "Cease fire!" when it got too close.

He came in with his first pass and started firing thousands of rounds. The rounds started chewing up the foliage and churning up the ground. The chopper got closer and closer until the fire was a few feet from us. I yelled, "Cease fire!" He had to be close, because we were fighting fifteen or twenty feet away. I think he made a couple of more passes before I heard a jet circling.

The pilot came on the radio and asked me where I wanted the seven hundred and fifty pound bomb placed. The last thing I wanted was for it to be dropped on top of us, which had happened to a company in the battle of Dak To. I tried to have it dropped a little over a hundred feet in front of us. I waited for it to come. I heard the jet coming and prayed it would not hit us. The jet released the bomb and there was a huge explosion. I was stunned by the concussion and had the wind knocked out of me for the moment.

I knew I was on a roll. I wanted to do the same thing on the other side of the perimeter. Out of the blue, several voices came on the air, making it impossible for me to communicate with the pilots. I think it was the top brass talking with each other. I started yelling and cussing at them to get off so I could continue, but they ignored me. By that time the incoming fire had slackened greatly, and then I saw the captain crawling by on his hands and knees toward the dust off area.

A couple of men had been able by that point to jump into the hole and get him out. We all started to back out of there, carrying the wounded as we went. There were thirteen dead, and, according to the medic, everybody in my platoon except for three were wounded or killed. I later heard that a platoon sergeant had gone crazy on the radio. I think they may have been referring to me.

We all pulled back about a hundred yards and dug in while the wounded were being evacuated. My squad had suffered two dead, and everyone was wounded except for me. There was no doubt about it—we had gotten our asses kicked, and the ones who survived were damn lucky to be alive. Most of the men in my squad had been flown out to the hospital, except for two who refused to leave. They were wounded by shrapnel and could have been flown out to safety, but they wanted to stay the night with me, despite my urging them to go. The enemy knew we were the only G.I.s in the area, and we were few.

It was almost certain that we would be attacked again that night. It brought tears to my eyes that the two men, knowing this, chose to stay. I was touched and I was grateful.

It was suddenly very dark and quiet, except in my ears, which were ringing from the roar and explosions during the battle. Ammunition had been flown in to us plus a machine gun for every position. Some positions had overhead cover (dirt and logs), but ours did not. We felt we could fight better without it. A new company commander had been flown in to temporarily take over for the wounded captain who had been flown out. He had been with us as a lieutenant before, and nobody liked him because of his disrespect for enlisted men. Less than half of our company remained, less than forty men, and we would be spending the night. We were told that if we could hold out until morning, we would be relieved by hundreds of paratroopers from the 101st Airborne.

We put all the machine gun ammunition boxes side by side at each position, linking them all together so the belt would feed the gun continuously for two thousand rounds without having to be reloaded. We had sixty-five full magazines of M16 ammo in boxes dug into the mound so they were easy to reach. We also had forty grenades in ammo boxes buried in the mound. We had bottles of lubricant in our pockets to keep our bolts lubricated if heavy fighting occurred.

As we sat in our fighting positions, I realized that again I had North Vietnamese fecal matter on my face from crawling around during the battle. It smelled terrible and was making me gag. I was in a state of psychological numbness, completely exhausted and in a state of shock thinking about the loss of so many friends and how badly we had been chewed up.

I was also very angry at the company commander for leading us right into the middle of a deadly ambush by following a trail which in the past we had always avoided, especially when we heard voices ahead. We were obviously being led by the enemy straight into their trap. Knowing we were greatly outnumbered, we could have flanked them or exercised alternative options rather than be led to our deaths. I felt that the company commander had been careless as we charged forward. Sure, it was our job to fight, but the way we did it was suicide. He had no regard for our lives. Actually, our company of ninety men never should have been sent there in the first place to fight an enemy that outnumbered us over three to one, and we had no artillery support.

All that night we could hear the enemy rummaging through the weapons and equipment we had left behind. They were also stripping the bodies for equipment, clothing, and boots, but, to our surprise, they did not attack.

In the morning there were some air strikes brought in, followed by an attack of the 101st Airborne. At that point the battle was essentially over, and, as we moved back into the battle area to gather up the dead, we ran into no resistance. Everything left behind had been taken by the NVA, and the bodies had been stripped.

While the job of putting our guys in body bags was going on, I looked over the area. We had walked into a perfect horseshoe ambush. The enemy had barbed wire and fighting positions. On both sides and in the front they had bunkers and tunnels, with sniper positions in the trees. There were North Vietnamese bodies all over the place.

We carried our dead back to the med-evac area to be flown out. The four South Vietnamese scouts who had been killed were flown out separately to different locations. We carried our bodies to the location at which we had spent the night. I sent my two wounded men suffering from shrapnel to be flown to the hospital in the rear area. My friend Wade wanted to stay with me. He refused to go despite his shrapnel wound and the pain it caused.

The lieutenant put Wade and I in charge of the dead bodies, making sure they got back to our rear area, over two hundred miles away, for processing. After a battle the dead were usually separated from the survivors, but not in this case. It was a blow to morale to have the survivors hanging around the dead. Wade and I loaded them onto two helicopters to be dropped off at some air force base somewhere. We escorted them there and then had to wait over twenty-four hours to catch a flight back to our battalion base camp.

We stayed with the bodies the whole time. We slept with them, and we ate beside them. They were beginning to smell really bad, but that was okay because they were our friends. Extremely exhausted, we had mud and shit all over us, and we were covered with the blood of our friends who had died during the battle. Our last flight involved cramming the bodies onto an aircraft to fly them to Tuy Hoa AFB, and then loading them onto a truck to be taken over a fifteen-mile bumpy dirt road to the morgue tent at our base camp.

The stretchers were too long and hung over the tailgate. One of us had to ride in the back of the truck with the bodies to make sure nobody fell out along the way. My friend wasn't too hot about riding in the back, so I told him it was okay if he rode in the cab. During the rough trip, I kept the bodies from falling off the truck. It was dark and almost daybreak. The moonlight coupled with the tossing back and forth of the truck made it look like the men in the bags were moving and alive. I caught myself mumbling and trying to talk to them.

There was a period during the firefight when I felt a fraction of an inch from death. For a few moments I had experienced a strange reality. It was a sensation of being aware of everything around me and of my life which flashed before me, separating the petty from the meaningful. It was a time of understanding and acceptance of death and a feeling of peace right in the middle of all the mayhem. Death was at reach; it was so close, but it required suffering a painful transition first. I experienced an unveiling of my spirit and soul. Just exactly what came over me for those few moments I can't accurately put into words. All I know is that it was spiritual. I was thinking that the dead had experienced an adventure that I had not; strangely I had a feeling of missing out.

Wade and I unloaded the bodies and carried them into the tent. We were told to wait outside and that we would be called in to identify them and sign the paperwork. We sat on a little dirt mound near the tent, waiting. We were exhausted with blood and shit all over us and watched as a couple of Jeeps full of officers pulled up and walked inside the tent. They seemed to be in there for a long time. The only reason I could think of for them wanting to go inside was that they wanted to gawk at the bodies like people stopping to rubberneck at a fatal accident scene.

They made us wait as we sat trembling. No one came over to see how we were doing, nor did they offer their condolences. We were simply two animals left over from the slaughter. We had our weapons with us as we always did in all situations, and I remember thinking about putting my selector switch on fully automatic and blowing them away. I, of course, would not have done that, but I did give it some thought.

I think most of us realized that America fighting in this war was insanity. North Vietnam wanted South Vietnam; that was obvious. I'm quite sure, as demonstrated by history, that the "domino effect" was nonexistent. There was no threat to the United States, and the government knew it. We were there for some other reason, but we didn't know what it was. Maybe money was the reason. Some people back home were making money from the war.

It was clear to us that the indigenous population was uneducated and just wanted to grow rice and survive. There was no justification for our involvement over there or for sixty thousand U.S. soldiers dying along with all the suffering of the thousands of wounded. Imagine too, the suffering of families, mothers, fathers, wives, and children. If we were fighting for America, as most of us believed, it would have been a completely different story. I think most of us doing the fighting had a new awareness of this war and also knew there was nothing we could do about it except try to protect each other, keep our heads low, and try to survive.

At the morgue we were greeted by our friend Smith, who was our supply man from the rear and former squad member. He was in a Jeep. The men in the bags were also his friends, having humped the boonies with him in the past. We hugged each other, and I could tell he had been crying prior to his arrival. He was upset, not only because the men in the bags were his friends, but also because he was not with us during the battle to do his part. We told him, "No sweat." We said that we were glad he had a safe job and that he always took good care of us when he flew in for re-supply.

The three of us, for the next three hours, identified bodies. They would take one out of a bag and sit it up against a center tent pole. The men in the bags looked horribly gruesome. Just the expressions on their bloody faces and the flies crawling in their open dead eyes were too much to look at. Again, there was the nagging, recurring question of why and how this could be justified in this war of nonsense and lies.

After the three of us were finished, we jumped in the Jeep and took Wade to the hospital tent. A nurse wanted to see his wound, at which point he took off his pants to reveal a hole in one of his butt cheeks surrounded by different rings of discoloration. It looked like a bull's-eye. I don't know where it came from, but a laugh came out of us. The nurse said he would have to stay to get the shrapnel removed, so we said goodbye and good luck. Smith and I then found for ourselves a safe outside bunker where we drank beer, ate some food, smoked opium, cried off and on, and finally passed out. I didn't think I would be missed by anyone at the company because everything was in such a state of disarray.

The next day I was able to clean up and eat some food. At that point I seriously started to worry about my mental health. I felt close to going crazy, but I realized the rest of my squad would be depending on me. Besides, there was nowhere to go for help. I think about half of our company were in the hospital, so it took about three weeks to reorganize.

During that time, the battalion commander got us together for a pep talk. As he stood there in his shined shoes, he told us that the G.I.s working the area of the battle had found well over two hundred dead and several fresh graves. He congratulated us on doing a fine job. Then he had the balls to tell us that it was rough to lose friends but what a glorious ultimate sacrifice. The muffled laughter was audible, but it had little effect on the man.

He then told us we would soon be back in the field convincing the enemy, who were returning in large numbers, to lay down their arms. Again, there was a response of muffled laughter. I think his face got a little red with anger—it certainly wasn't humility; he ended his speech and walked away. The lieutenant, who we called "the village idiot," did what I had told him to do, which was to try not to call in air strikes. Shortly after, he was relieved of duty and transferred somewhere else. He just disappeared. Maybe they were pissed off because he didn't take over and call in the strikes like an officer should do.

After any big battle there is a frenzy, I'm sure, of officers trying to receive medals for valor. I wrote up two of the men in my squad for Silver Stars and dropped off my request at the company headquarters. The first sergeant, who was rarely in the field, told me that he would take care of it. I think my requests were thrown in the trash because it was protocol that only officers recommended people for medals, mostly themselves.

I learned later that our company commander, who had led us right into the ambush and then spent the whole time during the battle in a well (that I believed he jumped into for cover), received the second highest medal, a Distinguished Service Cross. The lieutenant who had flown in and taken over for him after the battle wrote him up for this huge medal, according to what the captain wanted him to say, and turned it in. This officer was not at the battle; he did not know what had happened or what the captain had done. He didn't interview any of the troops about it; he just wrote it up as truth. What also bothered me was that all the big brass in the rear knew that I was on the radio calling in air strikes, not the captain. But as partners in a lie, they went ahead and decorated him anyway.

I have always done just fine not having any recognition for saving everybody's asses, including my own, but what troubles me is the lie told by the captain and the other officers involved in this medal, which would later catapult him into a high-ranking military career—all based on a lie. I know what I did, and others knew what I did, and I truly am okay with that.

I often wonder how he lives with himself and how the officers were able to so easily pull this off. Officers were educated, gentlemanly, important people with high status. They are the real focus in the military, and it is my opinion that they grabbed all the credit they could from the enlisted men, who did the brunt of the fighting and took most of the major casualties.

In general, the officers were a private, elite brotherhood of the privileged and entitled who lived off the backs of the low class, hard-working, obedient, unnoticed, and expendable enlisted men. To fraternize with enlisted men was a sin. Officers never learned how to gain respect from the men under them probably because the enlisted men were never shown the same respect. They never learned how to bring out the best in the men under them. The high medals went to the officers, and the few lower medals went to the enlisted men. In all fairness, it is my understanding that other branches of the military treated their enlisted men much better. It was the army that had this big problem.

But, again, the captain has to live with the fact that he didn't deserve that medal and in fact should have been in trouble for his tactical blunder that got a bunch of my friends killed. Sure, it was his job to fight the enemy, but to do it in a way that was so blatantly careless was beyond irresponsible.

# - 19 -

# BACK TO WORK

After about a week in the rear, we got brand-new replacements. I received six new people, plus two of my regular squad members who had just gotten out of the hospital. The word came down that our battalion was developing a reconnaissance platoon, and volunteers were sought. One of my two experienced men decided to volunteer, thinking he would not have to fight the major battles and that his chances of going home were better. So he left with all of our blessings. That left me with one experienced man in my squad and the rest untested. This meant that my squad would be pulling ranger element, which is a squad that leads the company about three hundred meters ahead. The idea was to scout ahead, pick the best route to travel, discover booby traps, and cut a trail. This was always very dangerous duty.

There was a lack of experienced squad leaders after the last battle, and I was one of the few people able to do this function. So instead of doing it once every nine days, I was doing it about every three days. The whole idea of this ranger element was that if it got hit, it would give the company time to maneuver. Our platoon also got a new lieutenant to replace the village idiot who they had gotten rid of. This lieutenant was a nice man, unlike the other officers.

One day my ranger element was moving up a dry river bed when I heard voices ahead. I was getting to be a "short timer," which meant that I didn't have long before I would be going home. You couldn't cheat on ranger because you had to keep moving forward, regardless of signs of the enemy. I called the company commander on the radio and told him there were voices ahead. He said that I had a choice: either my ranger element could move ahead to check it out, or he would bring the company up to us for support. He then said that the company, due to the number of men, would probably make a bunch of noise and eliminate our advantage over the enemy, who did not know we were there.

I decided to check it out without the rest of the company. We moved ahead slowly until we were about fifty feet from a little plateau just above. I told my squad that I would move up alone, to avoid the squad being detected, and check out the situation. They agreed to cover me as I moved along the trail and got into firing position. My heart was in my throat as I slowly moved about three feet to one side of the trail. Suddenly, I saw a person walking down right toward me. I was behind a bush, my M16 was on fully automatic, and I was about to blow the bastard away, when I noticed it was a woman. She was older, maybe fifty or sixty, and had not noticed I was there. She stopped at a bush right ahead of me, turned around, and relieved herself. I hesitated shooting her because I speculated that she was with a small family of people hiding from the war, merely trying to survive.

When she was through she wiped herself with what appeared to be a handful of leaves and started back up the trail. I then ordered her in Vietnamese to come to me. She took off running back up the hill where she had come from. There was a commotion on the plateau of people scrambling. I could not kill this old woman, but I did open up on either side of her as she ran because I didn't know what was there. At that point we all charged up the hill. Whoever was there were all gone. There were small crude animal traps, some freshly picked fruit, and a few other odds and ends. I was right. It was just a small group of refugees trying to live, and they posed no threat to us.

When the rest of the company moved up to us I explained what happened. The company commander was furious with me that I had not shot this woman. I don't remember my exact response to him, but it had something to do with living with myself if I survived long enough to go home. He made it clear after that experience that he did not like me. I didn't think he liked anybody anyway, and I didn't give a rat's ass.

A couple of days later, our platoon was in the rear of the company when everybody stopped for some reason. The company was waiting for something, as it sometimes did, when a few M16s up ahead started firing. We didn't know what was going on until the captain reported on the radio that a Viet Cong soldier (VC) had been killed, and he was propping him up so the new guys in the company could see his body. What had happened was, while the company was moving along the trail next to a long steep hill, they heard someone coming down the hill toward them and stopped.

They waited for the VC to appear, and then they blew him away like a firing squad. The guys who shot him later said that his eyes were as big as saucers. The company continued on moving past the body for the new guys to see. I guess it was supposed to be educational.

Our company was later involved in a huge operation along with the Korean and South Vietnamese soldiers called the "rock crush." According to intelligence reports, there was a large number of enemy concentrated in one area. The plan was that everybody, the Koreans, the South Vietnamese battalion, and our company, would form a huge circle surrounding the enemy. This circle would move slowly about a hundred yards each day toward the middle to trap the enemy. I was thinking that this was going to be a stupid circular firing squad. If we made enemy contact, we would all be shooting each other. This operation was like a vacation for us though, because we only had to hump all that weight a very short distance toward the middle each day. The operation lasted for about a week with a massive number of soldiers coming together in the middle. We found nothing but one old lady and a skinny cow. The operation must have been a major embarrassment to the big brass.

After that, it took days to airlift all those troops out of there and back to their own areas of operation. Wouldn't you know, our platoon was the very last to be flown out.

The old lady was flown out for interrogation. We killed the cow and had a barbecue.

Our drinking water was coming from a stream. There was a problem, however, because the Koreans were just upstream taking baths, and the water tasted like soap. We were drinking their dirty bath water.

The meat we barbequed smelled good, but it was as tough as shoe leather and just about impossible to eat.

Several helicopters came in and hovered while the last of us formed small groups and jumped on to fly off. Out of nowhere, over the noise of the chopper, we started hearing incoming rounds popping and whizzing right through the open doors of the helicopter as we took off. At first the door gunner was not aware that we were receiving incoming fire. There were no targets to be seen, so we just blasted away as we flew off. It was a miracle that not one of us got hit by this incoming fire. We were scratching our heads and wondering where in the hell this enemy came from, because the area had been thoroughly searched. Obviously, they were all concealed underground the entire time.

As I mentioned, I was a short timer and getting shorter every day. The shorter I got, the more scared I got. I knew two men who got killed their last day in the field. The new lieutenant, who I really liked (what a rarity), was able to get me out of the field a little early because a sergeant who had extended for another tour of duty—which was totally beyond my comprehension—was returning after a thirty-day leave back in the States. I did not understand him at first because he seemed to be more scared than I was. I found out later that many men extended because the war had screwed them up so badly they no longer had a home back in the states. That is, they couldn't fit in anymore. In four days I would be catching a re-supply helicopter down in the rice paddies to be flown back to the rear area to be processed out. So here I was with only four days left to hump out of the mountains and away from combat.

We had been playing cat and mouse with a battalion of NVA who had moved into the area, and we had discovered two large enemy base camps on each side of a river. As we walked through them, the NVA were busy going out the other side. They only fought us when they were ready, and thank God they were not. My last night in the field we had heard enemy mortars in the distance, and in the morning word came down that a company down in the rice paddies had been mortared. The enemy battalion was located along a dry riverbed about half a mile from the top of a mountain. Our company's orders were to go down that dry riverbed to try to find them. And wouldn't you know it, my squad would have point.

The sergeant who had returned to the company after he extended was to lead the ranger element in front of us. The ranger was supposed to be three hundred meters in front of my point, but the sergeant was scared and had asked me to keep him in sight at only about fifty meters. It would be our little secret. So here it was, my last day in the field, and my squad was to go right into the heart of an NVA battalion and probably get my ass killed. I could not have had any worse luck than that on my last day.

We arrived at the dry riverbed and started down the half mile hike. Halfway down we could smell them. There were bandage wrappers and other debris where they had sustained some of our artillery the night before. I think they were there on either side of us as we proceeded down the riverbed. The captain ordered cloverleaf patrols on either side to try to make contact with them. My squad was ordered to go to the right about a hundred meters, do a cloverleaf, and return.

As we were leaving, the captain told me, "Hey, Sergeant Roberts, if you come back with a mortar tube, it will be a big feather in your cap." I muffled something like, "Look for the fucking mortar tube yourself." He was the one who would get that feather if we captured it, not me.

We started off. I wasn't at all motivated to follow orders and get myself and my squad killed, so we moved out about fifty meters and stopped. We just squatted down for a while and returned. None of the squads that did a cloverleaf patrol made contact with the NVA. Maybe they all did the same thing that my squad did, I don't know. I don't understand why they didn't hit us on the way down, but I'm happy they didn't. When our company reached the bottom where the rice paddy was, there were empty enemy foxholes along the wood line at the edge of the mountain.

The helicopter came in with supplies, and after they unloaded, I said goodbye to my squad, wished them all luck, and flew off to the rear area to safety. I had never been so relieved and happy in my life, and I remember pissing a little bit in my pants. I was so fucking happy that I would live; I was out of my mind. Then I started thinking about the new guys I had left behind, and I knew that some of them would not live to go home and enjoy the same feeling I was experiencing. So I sat in the chopper with heavy guilt, sadness, and feelings of euphoria all at the same time. What was the point of them dying? How could it be justified?

When we got to the rear area, I immediately heard that "A" Company went up the hill in the same place that our company had just come down, and they got hit pretty hard. That was all I knew or cared about knowing. My friend Smith, who worked in the rear, was there to greet me. The next day my friend and I spent some party time in his bunker.

While I was walking to headquarters to see if I could get a change of clothes and start the process of going home, I was pretty preoccupied with those thoughts and happened to walk past an officer without saluting. He yelled at me, "Hey, troop! Don't you believe in saluting officers?" I tried to apologize, but he got right in my face and demanded that I shut up and stand at attention.

The next thing I knew, I had him by the shirt and was going to hit him with my right hand. He went into a squat with one arm up, trying to protect himself when two enlisted men pulled us apart. I just walked away saying to myself, "Holy shit! What have I just done!" The next day I heard not a word about it.

# - 20 -

# GOING HOME

My orders to return to Fort Bragg, North Carolina, had been processed, and I was on my way to catch the "freedom bird" back to the states for a thirty-day leave. I said goodbye to Smith. He would also be going home himself. We made arrangements to meet in the States after we were discharged, and then I was off, headed to someplace near Saigon to fly home.

Most of the soldiers returning home on the plane were very quiet. One would think they would be celebrating, but they were not. After two days of flying, on Friday the 13th (because of the time zones), I would land at a base in Washington state where a steak dinner would be provided to the troops coming home. The steak dinner consisted of a chow line in which we received a six ounce steak cooked how we wanted it. It was a nice gesture. We were told before boarding our respective planes to remember to watch our language because we were back in civilization. That was the only preparation we received before going home.

Going home and meeting my family at the L.A. airport (LAX) was wonderful. What a culture shock that was, being right out of a combat zone into civilization. During my thirty days on leave, I caught up with all the foods that I had craved for a year. I gained back about twenty-five pounds and felt very well physically. I also caught up on hot showers and all the other good things in life. On the downside, I was having major problems trying to sleep. I evaluated every little noise during the night. My sisters commented that I could hear and smell things long before anyone else.

It bothered me that no one understood what was going on in Vietnam. Many of the people I met in my home town, old friends and others, did not really care about what was going on in the war, even though at that time over two hundred soldiers were dying every week.

I was also suffering from hyper-vigilance, always in a state of being ready for something to happen. In general, there was an intensity about me that was not there before I left for the war. My soul was not intact. I had changed. I really didn't say anything to my family, because I didn't want them to worry about me. To them I was a war hero, and they were so proud of me. I tried to put on a good face and get on with my life.

At that time I had about six months left in the service, but I would put in for an early out to start college. My mother appealed to our congressman to see if he could make that happen.

When I got back to Fort Bragg, I was truly amazed. Before I left, Fort Bragg was completely different. Wherever you walked, whatever you did, you had to be perfect in manner and dress or else you would be dropped for push-ups. The environment was very military—very strict and very difficult. We were part of the mighty 82nd Airborne Division, and we had to be looking "strike."

After returning, I saw that the whole operation had unraveled. Half the soldiers were out of uniform, and many would not even get out of bed in the morning to make it to general muster, where everybody is supposed to be up in uniform and accounted for. I couldn't believe how that place had changed in a period of one year. The men coming back from Vietnam were for the most part rebellious, uncooperative, and on drugs or drunk. Lots of soldiers were out of control and just didn't give a shit.

The first sergeant whose role was to be the tough guy was now almost begging men to cooperate. He ended up putting me in charge of the very worst of the bunch in a desperate attempt to straighten them out. What he didn't realize was that I had the same sentiments about the army as the others did, and I wasn't getting much done either.

For training purposes, they wanted me to run up and down hills with a platoon playing war games and yelling, "Bang! Bang! Bang!" I explained that after what I and many of the other men had been through, I just couldn't do it. I also announced that I would not be making any parachute jumps either and that I wanted them to take me off the manifest. I didn't have it in my heart to do that stuff, and neither did anybody else. I was spent.

I told the first sergeant that I had about three months left, and then, if he wanted to, he could take away my sergeant stripes, or do whatever he wanted with me, but I couldn't play the game. He asked me if I could just do one thing with my time left: to straighten out and organize one filing cabinet. I told him I would do the best I could, but I wasn't even able to accomplish that, although I honestly did take a stab at it.

The interesting part about all of this was that the army didn't know what to do about it. They were at a total loss. I don't know if it was just my company or if the whole base was having problems. I finished out my last three months sitting around drinking beer and driving around in my car that I had purchased with the money I had saved in Vietnam.

We couldn't spend anything over there, so I was able to save almost everything I made. I was supposed to be home by Christmas, but the captain was so pissed-off at me that he delayed giving me my orders until after the holidays.

As I drove home, I sang as loudly as I could to the radio. Many times I felt like stopping the car and jumping as high as I could in the air. I was free, and I was alive! But my elation was mixed with acute sadness for those whose lives had been cut short and who would not be sharing my moment nor would I be sharing theirs.

# - 21 -

## THE BOYS' HOME

The boys' home where I got a job was located in an upper middle class neighborhood in Woodland Hills, a block or two away from a fancy country club nestled in the foot hills. It had a central dining room and kitchen, an administration building, and three separate cottages that held about twenty-five boys each. It sat on seven acres with big trees and had nicely kept grounds and very well-maintained structures. One cottage was home to the younger junior high kids, another to the kids in upper middle school, and the third was home to the high school kids.

These were kids placed by the court, kids who had gotten into trouble with the law. This was not a place for serious offenders. The serious offenders were placed with California Youth Authority. The kids at the home were bused to public schools and were free, within reason, to roam the community, go to movies, and more. The majority of the people in the neighborhood accepted the boys' home. I think it had been there long before most of the people had moved there, so it was pretty well-established.

If the boys were doing okay at school and following the rules, they could earn a little freedom and could make a little money by working in the kitchen if they chose. These boys were not considered incarcerated. There were no fences and no guards. If they wanted to run away they could easily do so, but when they got picked up they would be taken to juvenile hall and would probably be placed somewhere else. Some of the boys couldn't make it at the home, got into serious trouble, and would be moved on to California Youth Authority (CYA). Some would eventually go to prison.

This home had a board of directors, a social worker and house father in each cottage, and several counselors. It also had a visiting psychiatrist who dispensed psychotropic medications to the boys when deemed necessary. The boys had a variety of behavior problems and some of them were emotionally disturbed.

I was hired as one of the part-time counselors in one of the cottages. I was thought of as a respectable, hard-working college student and veteran of Vietnam. Had they known of my mental state they never would have hired me, but I put on the act of being a stable, patriotic person who might be a good mentor for the kids. In reality, it was a situation of the blind leading the blind. I did try, however, to do a good job. I made sure the boys were following their programs, and I provided some emotional security and stability in their lives. I could relate to them from my own wild and crazy days when I was their age. I thought I could make a difference.

It wasn't long before I discovered that this job was causing a major change in my life. I, like the other counselors, expected the kids to follow the program and obey the rules. But I also felt that I needed to develop a real relationship with these kids, more than just that of a custodian.

I had stumbled onto something big. Working with these kids was pretty demanding and necessitated my full focus. I found myself thinking outside of my own problems in reaching out to them. I fell in love with these kids and felt a personal responsibility to help them if I could. My involvement with them was helping me with my own problems. I was starting to feel better about myself, and I realized how healing it was for me to serve others. My work there directly fit into my studies of sociology and psychology; it was the perfect job for me.

I went from a jungle fighter who was very much a part of destruction and death to helping troubled youth. What an incredible transition and what a positive experience this was for me. I discovered that a helping profession was a possible career goal. When I was alone and away from the job and from my classes I was still having major problems with grief, sleeplessness, anxiety, depression, guilt, anger, thoughts of suicide—all with great intensity.

For the first time since I got out of the military, however, I thought there was hope for me. I decided that these problems and memories of the war were deeply etched in my brain, and I would have to live with them the best I could. They were going to be with me for a long time, but they were gradually becoming easier to bear.

I didn't know how other combat vets were doing since veterans did not seem to talk to each other or anyone else at that time. Was I alone in feeling cowardly and weak? Were other combat vets having the same problems? Little did I know that in just a few years the suicide rate among veterans would surpass the fifty-nine thousand actually killed in the war.

Little did I know that veterans all over the country were having major problems with post-traumatic stress disorder (PTSD). People back from Vietnam were trying to forget about their problems and get on with their lives, only for PTSD to hit them right between the eyes. At that time, PTSD was not even a diagnosis. Veterans did not trust the government Department of Veterans Affairs (VA) and really did not know who to go to with their problems. The services through VA evolved very slowly and came into existence years later—sadly much too late for those who had taken their own lives.

Traditionally, this country rushes men into war and then moves like a snail when it comes to helping them when they come home. America is interested in all the glory stuff, making money and winning. Most everyone was interested in hearing the news of actual fighting during the war, but not very interested in seeing cripples, nor vets with psychological problems, nor homeless vets walking around among them. I mean, who would be interested in that? Don't look at the suffering; that is uncomfortable. Let's not spend too much time feeling sorry for families who are grieving. If we don't look, maybe it will all go away. Thank God things are getting much better for returning soldiers of our present wars.

For me the boys at the home were great. They did the damnedest things. For instance, late one night they quietly snuck a prostitute into the cottage. The staff heard about it the next day because the boys just couldn't keep it a secret.

Over a period of a couple weeks they stored food under the floor and then went on a hunger strike to protest something.

I don't remember what they were protesting, but the staff and the administration were worried because the kids were not going to the dining hall and eating. It appeared they were actually going hungry, but in reality they had stashed plenty of food back at the cottage under the floor which the staff later discovered. They couldn't keep that a secret either.

One time, the boys made wine out of fruit juice, sugar, and yeast they got from the dining hall. That was also manufactured beneath the floor of the cottage in a three-foot space between the floor and the ground.

During my time there, it was discovered that the boys were actually growing marijuana under the floor. None of the staff were able to keep the kids out of that space under the floor. They were always finding ways to sneak back under there to do their deeds. If they were caught, they would lose privileges for a while, depending on the violation, and would have to work off their points.

One evening, a counselor took about fifteen boys to the mall in our bus. While the counselor was inside the mall dealing with two boys who had been caught shoplifting, the others were out in the parking lot trying to hotwire the bus. They were not able to accomplish this feat, but they did manage to screw up the ignition so it wouldn't start when the counselor tried to take them back. The boys who had to stay behind back at the home urinated on the others' beds. When the boys returned and went to bed there was almost a riot. We had to get the sleeping bags from the camping room for them to sleep in the living room. One kid actually pissed in his own bed so he could get a sleeping bag and join the others.

The reason the boys were placed in the home in the first place had more to do with their dysfunctional families than anything else. They all had bad home lives and were acting out because of it.

The boys liked to go camping, so those who had earned the right to go would be treated to a few days at the beach. These boys mostly had lived in the Los Angeles inner-city area, so I also wanted to expose them to some challenging backpacking trips in the High Sierra.

The trip would involve a lot of planning and money for equipment such as backpacks and special footwear. The money had to be raised. Finally the director of the home came up with the money for the equipment. After special classes where I taught the boys about safety, how to never wander off alone, how to read a compass, how to ration their freeze-dried meals, how to stay warm, and how to keep their food from being eaten by the bears, we were ready for the trip.

We drove to nine thousand feet and stayed there to get acclimated to the elevation at a place called Onion Valley up above Independence. We then went higher on the switchbacks and up over Kearsarge Pass, which is almost twelve thousand feet. We stayed in the back country for about five days. The trip was hard and challenging, but they loved it and really rose to the occasion. So, after coming from the streets and alleys of Los Angeles, they got to experience the great outdoors. This trip was a hit and was the first of many such backpacking excursions.

I thought the boys' home was a wonderful institution. I made many friends and continued to work there for about three years until I somehow received my bachelor's degree in sociology. I wanted a master's degree, which necessitated a move to Fresno, and so, sadly, I would have to end my employment at the boys' home.

During my employment there, I lived in a garage and slept on a mattress on the floor. I hated to go home to this place, because time there was always spent in depression. One night I had a setback, got drunk, and passed out on my mattress. I woke up in the morning with my .30-30 Winchester on my chest and cartridges around me. Apparently I had been in the process of loading the rifle to shoot myself when I passed out.

I was horrified that morning because it was the closest I had ever come to killing myself. I immediately went to the pawn shop and got rid of the rifle. The reason I had a weapon in the first place was because it made me feel more secure. I don't know what other peoples' thoughts look like before they attempt to commit suicide, but mine were fixated on intoxication, depression, Vietnam-era music, my dead friends, and the power of the weapon I was going to use. I would wallow in all of this for a long time. The experience was like some evil meditation—the climax of which would be blowing my brains out. Luckily for me I was always interrupted before that last step, and my suicide attempts never came to fruition.

# - 22 -

# CULTURAL REVOLUTION

During the first period of my college years, I was quiet as a mouse about being a veteran because I knew I would be persecuted to some degree and be treated like an unwanted misfit. The Vietnam War was unpopular, and veterans were representative of that. One time in a college class the subject came up, and it was announced that over two hundred American soldiers were being killed every week. I remember someone in the class laughing, as if the soldiers deserved it. There was a general attitude of indifference at best. I remember wanting to speak out, but nothing would come out of my mouth. I was frozen in rage, and the top of my head was about to blow off; I just got up and walked out. If I had stayed I don't know what would have happened.

Social science departments in colleges began answering the call by making their curriculum and class discussions geared more toward contemporary times. I remember someone passing a joint around in a philosophy class. I remember a professor being physically removed from a class by the students and told not to come back until he could do a better job. Institutions of authority—military, local governments, state and federal governments, justice and law enforcement institutions—were being morally challenged.

There was a cultural revolution going on all over the country. Young people under about thirty were shedding the values they had grown up with. Woodstock was roaring and music was undergoing major change. Songs were being written to reflect perfectly what was going on in American society. Young people adopted the philosophy of peace and love. There were social dropouts. Bare feet and long hair became the norm. Lots of women stopped shaving their legs and armpits in their quests to be free. The so-called "hippie" movement was starting to flourish.

There were antiwar demonstrations on almost every college campus. Watergate was going on, and many lost respect for government. Police were not to be trusted and were referred to as "pigs." The drug culture seemed well-established, and many young people were high all the time. They took LSD and could take trips without leaving home. There was a lot of personal experimenting with drugs, as people believed they were mind-expanding.

There was a popular book written by John C. Lilly called *The Center of the Cyclone*. He talked about taking massive amounts of LSD, floating naked in a dark tank, and having out-of-body experiences. It was a time of anything goes.

Militant groups were forming. There were the Black Panthers and the Brown Berets, and Native Americans organized the American Indian Movement (AIM). All of these groups were fighting back and hitting America right in the face for its long history of war-mongering, historical lies, and racial discrimination and injustices. There were many who believed that if it weren't for Martin Luther King, Jr., a follower of Gandhi who preached nonviolence during the social upheaval of the civil rights movement, we would have had a full-out race war.

It was a time for speaking out, seeking the truth, and demanding the country make good for its historical wrong-doings. The antiwar demonstrations all over the country were demanding an end to the war. National Guard troops were being called out to keep the peace. Four demonstrators were shot and killed at Kent State University on May 4, 1970. A giant counter-culture had emerged that would change the country forever. The establishment (mostly people over thirty) was freaking out and comparing all of this to the fall of Rome, thinking the country surely would not survive.

Despite the social unrest, the colleges and universities during this time were intact. They were trusted institutions; they were the centers of protest, and people were flocking to them. I have always maintained that the vehicle for the airing of national disputes and truth has always been professors and students in educational institutions, not the lying politicians in our state and federal governments, especially Congress. Not only do colleges and universities maintain and represent the hard and soft sciences, but they always seem to be on the cutting edge of the contemporary. They are the centers of open debate, unlike our political system, which is locked into competitive partisanship. It is too bad that what is discussed in college and university classes isn't covered by the media for all to learn.

During the years of unrest in this country, many interesting phenomena were developing. Spiritual growth and Eastern religious philosophies were drawing interest. Many people were practicing different kinds of meditation. Self-awareness and encounter groups were becoming popular.

Most encounter groups were small, consisting of about eight people. The groups generally would begin with the same ground rules, such as no violence, one person speaking at a time, no drugs or alcohol, confidentiality, a genuine caring of others, and exactly what time the meeting would end, which provided an incentive for people to make sure they said what they wanted to say. The groups would have a leader or facilitator (therapist, counselor, social worker, or psychologist). The leader was skilled and would control the group according to what he or she wanted to achieve, which was mostly, from my experience, to make him or herself look brilliant.

The purpose was group therapy. There was a need for people with problems to have a place to talk and gain acceptance. Individuals would offer support and insights about themselves and others as they went around the circle. The spirit of the whole thing was caring, honesty, and spontaneity, the gaining of self-awareness and knowledge about themselves through feedback from others.

These groups gained popularity very quickly. Many of the people I knew were involved in some sort of a group or other. There were sensitivity groups where people put oil on themselves, turned off the lights, and, in a tight circle, gently rubbed each other. When the lights came back on they would talk about their experiences.

Sometimes a loaf of bread would be passed around the circle. Each member would hold it, caress it, smell it for a while, take a small piece and let it melt in their mouth. The group would then talk about their heightened sensitivity and what they had experienced.

There were marathon groups that went all night long. The purpose was to make people break down from the intensity and out of exhaustion so that the real truth would reveal itself. Supposedly when this happened it was considered a major break-through and a life-changing experience.

People took these groups very seriously, including me. I participated in many of them. I remember hearing at the time that corporations and small businesses were starting to practice these types of group sessions. The thinking was to help employees achieve better, more honest communication and working relationships and thus benefit the company. Where else could someone have an audience and be validated on a regular basis other than in an encounter group? At first I thought I was getting a lot out of these groups, and then I came to realize it was all bullshit. Maybe not at first, but I think it turned into that.

After a few years, these groups seemed to evolve into something phony, entertaining and recreational. People acquired skills in the group process, learned the jargon, and started competing for control over individuals in the group and the group itself. Some participants even became popular and had reputations. They would pretend like they really had it all together. I noticed that some groups became more confrontational and some were mean-spirited. In this way, groups became a challenge for individuals to see how well they could hold their own against people who were bright, articulate, and receptive.

I took a sociology class once, and the professor was doing psycho-dramas off campus on Friday nights. I went to one out of curiosity. The purpose of the drama was to provide therapy for someone having a problem by changing roles back and forth while telling their story.

Here is how it worked: The professor was the director. About thirty to forty people would sit in a circle in a large room void of furniture except for two chairs placed in the middle. The director would go around the room and casually feel everyone out until he found a person with a problem. He would then ask this person to take the hot seat in the middle.

An example might be someone who was having difficulty dealing with their mother. The director would have a volunteer take the other seat and play the part of the mother. Then an alter ego would stand behind each chair and say things that they thought the person in the hot-seat wasn't saying. He would encourage the person in the hot seat to tell the mother all about why he thought he wasn't loved, why he was so angry at her, and why she had treated him so unfairly. Then, just at the right time, the director would say, "Switch roles." Seats were changed so that the troubled person would play the mother and have to respond to himself.

This changing of roles would go on until the person would break down and cry. At that point everyone would take their original seats, except the person crying. The director would stop the action and go around the audience asking them what they thought the problem was. He would then put his arm around the person, tell him exactly what his problem really was in a supportive way, and put him back together again and making sure he was all right, thus completing this miracle right before everyone's eyes.

One week a woman had rejected me. I had taken her out for dinner and then to a bar. She didn't drink much, but I did. Apparently I got a little weird, and she walked out on me. It left me very depressed and lonely. So I thought I would show up at the psychodrama and get to the bottom of it. The next week I was called to the hot seat. Without divulging any of my military experiences, I told the story of what happened in the bar.

We were going back and forth changing roles, and pressure was mounting because I wasn't breaking down. The director kept the pressure on me until I finally stopped the drama myself and said it just wasn't working. Then the audience started telling me what they thought the problem was. They were coming up with all kinds of shit that I knew wasn't true. Then the master himself put his arm around me and divulged the big secret. You could hear a pin drop as he shared his revelation. He said, "You are setting yourself up for rejection." I disagreed and said that wasn't right. As lonely as I was, that was the last thing I wanted to do. His response was, "See, you are doing it right now." Everything I said only reinforced his diagnosis of me "setting myself up for rejection." It got so bad I walked out to go home to face my depression once again. I knew in my heart he was wrong and that he had no right to do this to people. My depression turned to anger, and I thought he needed to be stopped. As badly as I wanted to kick his ass, I knew it would not serve my future well.

The next day I was drinking wine with my hippie friend who always wore a smelly leather serape and an English professor who had taken me under his wing. One of the requirements for his class was to write a journal about your life. Since it was confidential and he would be the only one reading it, I took a chance and wrote about Vietnam. He sensed I was a bombshell about to go off, so he befriended me to try to help me out and encouraged me to keep writing. Looking back on it, I give him credit for saving my life. After telling my companions what had happened in the psychodrama, we all three decided we should go together to the next one and disrupt the hell out of it.

Before we started, we drank a lot of wine. Then we loaded up in my friend's old Volkswagen, which only ran on three cylinders, and headed to the drama. It had already started when we arrived. The director was taken aback when he saw the English professor, and he overlooked us breaking his no alcohol rule. He knew the English professor, who had a reputation on campus for being a nonconformist radical. He was obviously intimidated by his presence when we walked in. Suddenly the director wasn't just dealing with dumb-ass students; he had a fellow professor in the midst watching him.

We started passing the gallon of wine around, which was violating the rules. As he directed the drama, the English teacher kept stopping him and correcting his English. My friend and I stopped the drama and started asking questions like, "Why are you people believing this man? Are you a bunch of sheep who can't think for yourselves? How do you know he is correct? Do you know that you and the director might be hurting people in these dramas?"

At that point, the director went ballistic, shaking his finger at us and screaming for us to get the hell out. The audience, following his lead, jumped angrily to their feet. There were some pretty strong-looking athletic types there who were his groupies and loyal to him. The group had turned into an angry mob. I had just read about mob behavior and made a gesture to my compatriots that we should get the fuck out of there! I think we were lucky to have made it to the car. We drove off feeling elated and doing victory yells in the night, knowing justice had been served and that we had prevailed. After that I don't think that professor ever held another psychodrama. I definitely felt better about it, and I was grateful to my friends who came to my aid.

# - 23 -

# EXTENDED FAMILY

My hippie friend with the leather serape dropped by the garage to talk to me. He knew I was depressed, and he wanted to talk me into renting a large house and starting an extended family. It took some real coaxing to get me out of my garage. Even though I hated the garage, I was very uncomfortable with the thought of living that closely to other people. But I told him I would try it to see if it might work out. Four students playing the part of being married were interviewed by the owner of this six-bedroom home across the street from the college. They rented the house, and all the students moved in. Each person had their own bedroom for privacy and a place to study. One student was majoring in political science, three of us were majoring in sociology, one girl was studying to become a teacher, and the other girl was majoring in psychology.

We had an organizational meeting in the living room to discuss the extended family idea and to establish the rules of the house. We decided that we wouldn't have any rules and that we would coexist in an atmosphere of respect for each other's privacy in a spirit of consideration. The only rule that we did have was to have a weekly meeting to discuss any problems or ideas that came up. We each had our own food in the refrigerator, which was respected by the others. One problem we had was friends coming over, smoking weed, and snacking on other peoples' food. Another problem was a big dog belonging to one of the girls. This dog would frequently shit in the kitchen. She didn't seem to mind, and this went on for a couple of weeks. We had a meeting and kicked her out.

To replace her, we ran an ad on the college bulletin board and interviewed applicants to join our extended family. This style of living was a lot less expensive than renting separate apartments, not to mention being a hell of a lot of adventure and fun. One of the applicants was named Joanne. While she was intelligent and sweet, I voted against her because I felt she was too innocent to live with us. I was outvoted, and she moved in. She fit in with our social science academic pursuits, majoring in psychology. She turned out to be a warm and wonderful person. She was an intelligent, sensitive, and gentle person who had been psychologically abused by her mother growing up.

I absolutely fell in love with this Italian girl who was warm, pretty, and had a body that wouldn't quit. I was not able to show any emotion when I talked to her. I was weird that way and practiced hiding my feelings, but I was crazy about her and decided to make a move. I asked her out and told her of my intentions, which were to take her to bed. Three times in a nice way she totally rejected me. I had to face the hard reality that she wasn't attracted to me. I got so frustrated that I moved to a tiny guest house one block down the street.

During the time that she and I lived at the house I had invited her to go backpacking. She agreed to go but still would not have anything to do with me romantically. How was I going to go backpacking in the wilderness with someone I was in love with who didn't care for me? I would be taking a few boys from the home with us, so I was hoping it wouldn't be too difficult for me. For a couple of weeks before the trip, I saw her carrying a backpack around the block in an effort to get in shape.

The day of the trip came and Joanne, the boys, and I took off in my truck toward Independence on the east side of the Sierra. We drove to Onion Valley at nine thousand feet, about half way up the mountain. We would stay there overnight to get acclimated to the elevation. The next morning we hiked off up the switchbacks with the goal of crossing over Kearsarge Pass, which was very close to twelve thousand feet and a very challenging hike. We hiked slowly, trying to move along at the slowest person's pace, which was Joanne's. We stopped to pick some wild onions along the trail to mix in with our freeze-dried dinners that night.

We reached the top of the pass at the Pinnacles where we could see close to a hundred miles; it was beautiful. We hiked down the other side of the pass to about ten thousand, five hundred feet and set up camp at a small lake along the trail. We were in the high country on top of the world. We set up our backpacking tents, ate supper, and got ready for a night of freezing temperatures. It was really nice having a lady that I was secretly crazy about along on the trip. Our plan for the rest of the week was to turn north and go up to a place called Sixty Lake Basin, which is an unbelievably beautiful area.

That night after dark, I checked on everybody and discovered that Joanne was starting to feel sick. The temperature had plummeted to below freezing. Her down sleeping bag was more than adequate, and she had a foam rubber mat that would insulate her from the cold ground. It was just a matter of her keeping warm and having water close to her. Still she was freezing cold and continued to get worse, experiencing nausea and a splitting headache. I was scared to death because I knew she was suffering from elevation sickness and hypothermia, both of which can be deadly. I guessed her body was exhausted, and I knew it was her first experience being at such a high elevation.

We had no cell phones in those days, and no emergency services. I knew a ranger station with the radio was up the trail about seven and a half miles, but I didn't know if the ranger would even be there. It was also dark as hell. The realization set in that this was a serious crisis. I had wanted to take her along on the trip, not realizing that it might be too much of a challenge for her as she was not an experienced backpacker. At the time she wanted to go, and all I could think about was how nice it would be having her along. My love for her and the desire to be around her clouded my judgment, and now she was in serious trouble. She could possibly die, and it was my fault.

I squeezed into her sleeping bag and put my sleeping bag over the top of us. The plan was to warm her up with my body heat and do whatever I could to take care of her and reassure her that she would be okay. That was really all I could do. I spent the night pressing my body against hers and rubbing her all over desperately trying to get her warm and keep her warm. Needless to say, I said a few prayers also. After a few hours she was comfortably warm, and in the morning she felt well enough to hike back down the mountain to go home. The boys understood, and I promised them that after we took her home, we would turn the truck right around and return to the mountains for a week's backpacking in the same area.

On the way home, she was very apologetic, feeling she had ruined the trip for everyone. I noticed also that she sat close to me and put her head on my shoulder. She expressed her extreme gratitude for saving her life, and I think she felt close to me for the first time. At the time I was just so grateful that she had survived the ordeal that I didn't give her affection much thought.

Back up in the mountains I did think about it. I felt good, and I couldn't wait to get back to see her. Two months later we were married under a four hundred and fifty-year-old oak tree with all our hippie friends in attendance. It was a joyous occasion. Our wedding and honeymoon cost less than three hundred dollars. She shared the same penchant as I to be frugal.

She tried hard to understand my problems and knew that I would always be there for her. Even though I wasn't sure inside that I would make a good husband and family man, I promised her I would try as hard as I could. Boy! I was the luckiest bastard in the world! We finished up our bachelor's degrees and went to another university to obtain our master's in rehabilitation counseling, going through the whole program together.

# - 24 -

# GRADUATE SCHOOL

T he master of arts in rehabilitation counseling was a two-year program consisting of three semesters of coursework and one semester of full-time internship in some institution. My internship was at a local community college that had just started a program providing supportive services to disabled students.

A new federal law called the Rehabilitation Act mandated that disabled students have access to vocational programs. State regulations followed that mandated access to community colleges and the setting aside of money from the state school fund in Sacramento to pay for services, which included: access to personal, academic, and vocational counseling; note-takers; interpreters for the hearing impaired; tutoring; mobility assistance; transportation; special testing arrangements; and whatever a disabled person needed to provide them with a level playing field and an equal opportunity to succeed in college.

Like non-handicapped people they could realize their dreams, acquire good jobs, and become independent, productive, and employed tax-paying citizens. These programs were cost-effective in that when these students became employed, they would more than pay back the cost of their rehabilitation through the taxes they would pay to the state and federal governments. It would also remove them from the public dole.

About the same time of this legislation, the Americans with Disabilities Act was passed, requiring institutions to remove physical barriers, replacing them with ramps and modified bathrooms, as well as providing other access rights. The timing of this legislation and my rehabilitation counseling master's degree landed me a job as director of disabled student services at a community college. My wife landed a job at the State Department of Rehabilitation. Later she also went back for another degree in special education and became a full-time teacher at a small elementary school.

The college where I worked was located in a small town nestled against the foothills of the Sierra Nevada mountains about a hundred and seventy-five miles from the Pacific Ocean. The first thing I learned at the college was that football and basketball were very important. Instead of the local boys playing for the college, the administration spent a lot of money to recruit athletes from all over the country. The college wanted to win. A good football and basketball team was like an extension of the administration. The administrators competed through their athletes against other administrators at other colleges in California. I guess the recruiter painted a rosy picture of our little town because one kid showed up with a surfboard. He said he was told the beach was ten minutes away.

I think all of the athletes recruited were black, and mostly from Oklahoma. The sad thing was that the town only had a few black residents. There was no African American culture to speak of and no particular neighborhood or place in town where these athletes could socialize. They were isolated. Unfortunate also was that the town was dominated by white, Bible Belt rednecks, and although they were not particularly demonstrative about it, they were not accommodating to black people. These students were just not wanted in the community. If the team was winning, everything was great, but when they were losing there were racial slurs and ugly language yelled out at them by the citizens in the stands. This was thirty-five years ago, and I surely hope things are different now.

The professors and students from the area were good to them, though. They were emotionally supported for the most part and were given jobs on campus. The good thing was, because it was an agricultural area half of the population was Hispanic. The black and hispanic cultures were more accepting of one another, and the athletes on some level were able to have social activities and interaction. I think the athletes' plans were to use the college as a stepping-stone to playing professionally and to be picked up by the NFL or NBA. This happened for only one student that I heard of, and since most of them were not great students they eventually moved on. A few got jobs and stayed in the community. These kids were friendly and I liked them. I always suspected the college had exploited them.

On my way to work one morning, I saw a car in an intersection with a dent in the front of the hood, a cracked windshield, and a big crimp on the top starting at the windshield and going to the back. In the front lay a crumpled bicycle. I stopped to learn that a huge linebacker had been hit by a car and went over the top. My heart stopped until I learned that he was scraped up but had no injuries. It would have been a great story in the paper that a linebacker on a bike went one on one with a car and the car lost. These guys were that big and strong.

My job was perfect for me. It allowed me a lot of professional latitude, and I loved it. It gave me freedom to creatively develop unique services for disabled students so they could succeed academically, vocationally, and in their personal lives. Don't get me wrong, they earned these things through their hard work, talent, and determination. My job was to make sure they had the opportunity to achieve through legally-mandated access to the college and supportive services.

Spiritually, my job was a continuation of the work I had done at the boys' home and of my own healing through service to others. It made me focus on others and removed me from my own problems. The college had no idea how screwed up I was nor the extent of my experiences. All they knew was that I had been in the Vietnam War and was just a hard-working, patriotic citizen. They knew I wasn't like those demonstrating, pot-smoking, hippie freaks.

I was living in a redneck, extremely politically-conservative area. I hid my true antiwar feelings and counterculture interests. I had to look and carry myself like a typical college professor (according to their standards) to survive. I had to be very careful until I received tenure, which would provide me with academic freedom and locked-in job security. After tenure, the only way I could lose my job was to be arrested for a felony.

After a couple years I did receive tenure and was able to enjoy more latitude, comfort, and freedom in my work. Within reason, I could feel comfortable being my true self. I had always worked hard, but now I didn't have to worry about some administrator unfairly victimizing or firing me, because I now had legal rights as a faculty member.

I was also enjoying the protection of a great teachers' union and had excellent medical insurance for the first time. I was advised to go to the Sansum Clinic in Santa Barbara to try out my insurance. I got a complete physical exam, including my first colonoscopy. I didn't know at the time that this was to be the most humiliating experience of my life.

I was a little worried about the five-foot hose they were going to insert into me. I was told that a person has five feet of colon, and they wanted to take a look at all of it. The office in the building had just been moved and had not yet been remodeled. The nurse took me to a prep room on the other side of the waiting room, and I was given a gown and the first of three enemas. After I relieved myself I would ring a bell. The nurse repeated this procedure two more times. Then I was told to walk through the waiting room to the exam room. I had to walk sideways past all the people in the waiting room because my ass was sticking out of the gown.

The procedure was easy, but the doctor must have pumped enough air in me to fill a truck tire. After the procedure I was told to again go through the waiting room to get dressed and then to go see my doctor. As I was crossing the room sideways with my ass hanging out, I started having the worst flatulence of my entire life. With each step sideways, there was a constant whining blast coming out of me. I must have done this thirty times. The people waiting tried to ignore it, but some, as hard as they tried to hold back, started laughing.

After getting dressed I saw the doctor, who told me there was one more test he wanted to do that required one more blood sample and that he needed to see me the next morning. I agreed, but since I was too far from home I had to stay in a motel across the street. I had been fasting the whole day, and I stopped by the cafeteria to pig out before going to the motel.

I had just about finished registering at the motel when I felt strong cramps coming on. I hurriedly grabbed the key to the room because I knew I didn't have much time. The cramps got stronger, and I began to panic because I was having trouble finding the room. I knew I was going to cut loose when I saw my room number upstairs. I knew I had just a few seconds, and I went flying up the stairs. I was in so much of a panic, I had trouble unlocking the door. Finally it opened and I raced to the bathroom. It was dark and I couldn't find the light switch, but I could see the outline of the toilet.

I hopped over to it, taking my pants down at the same time, sat down, and exploded. "Oh my God!" The toilet seat was down with that paper strip across it. I shit all over myself and the bathroom. Fecal matter was in my shoes, in my underwear, in my pants, socks, and shirt. My wallet was even wiped out. I got in the shower and then called my wife. She said to calm down and to try to relax. She told me to wash everything out and let it dry overnight. Anyway, I cleaned everything up and survived.

# - 25 -

# STUDENT STORIES

I fell in love with my students and had many faculty and classified friends, but I became a thorn in the side of the administrators. I didn't like them telling me what to do, exercising authority over me—as they thought was their mission— and assuming that they knew more about my specialty than I did.

I was surprised and disappointed with some of my colleagues who genuinely thought disabled students were inferior and should not be at the college. One instructor used to lock the door exactly when his class was scheduled to begin. A disabled student was going as fast as he could on forearm crutches from the other side of campus to get to his class. Just as he got to the door this instructor, watching him through the door window, locked the door and looked at him like, "Tough shit, buddy." I think if there was ever a reason to kick somebody's ass, this was the one. I was so beside myself with anger that I cannot recall what I said when I went to his office to talk to him.

Some of the other instructors were also slow to accept the new state and federal regulations. These were the same professors with whom I had to work out deals for academic modifications like a variety of special testing arrangements, oral testing, more time on tests, note-takers, student aids, having to move classrooms because of accessibility, and more. My students suffered from physical, learning, and psychological disabilities.

Some professors were locked into protocol and stereotypes about the disabled and had elitist attitudes about their teaching methods. Generally, professors caught on and were understanding and eager to work with disabled students, as long as the students could prove and demonstrate that they were learning the material. The instructors learned that even a person in a wheelchair, who perhaps couldn't speak, actually had a brain and was just as smart, or smarter, than so-called "normal" people.

There were a few exceptional instructors like Bev Richardson from the English department, who was wonderful, and Walt Snyder, who taught history, geology, and geography. Walt was an extremely difficult instructor with the highest of academic standards. If students were going to succeed in his class they had to work their asses off, and that included disabled students. Walt was one of the few who treated them with respect and was more than willing to modify his methods for disabled students to provide a level playing field.

Even though he was academically difficult, my students excelled in his classes. The disabled students could even take advantage of overnight field trips, which were a joint collaboration between Tom Howell, chair of the art department, who took his photography students, and Walt, who took his geography and geology students for field work to places like Death Valley and Zion National Park. My students were able to participate on these trips with the use of my program's handicapped bus along with the very genuine support of Tom, Walt, and all of the students on the trips. Indeed, these trips became the highlight of the semester for many of my students.

Students in wheelchairs had told me about those in the community who refrained from looking at them, as if they weren't there. They also experienced people talking baby talk to them. Some would speak very loudly to them, assuming, I guess, that they were all deaf. These students also were met sometimes with the subtle attitude that they were being punished by God for some great sin they or their parents must have committed.

In working with them I did not baby them or want to be their protector. Through counseling, I wanted them to make their own decisions, learn to fight for their rights, and feel good about themselves. Often a student would come into the office and say that they had no idea what they wanted to do. I would tell them to come back when they had some ideas. Most of them had some ideas about what they wanted to pursue. They were damn tough already and only needed my help to set up some supportive services. I had great respect for them. The last thing they wanted was pity or sympathy.

One time I had a blind student who wanted to learn carpentry. The college offered a carpentry class that actually built a house each semester, right there on campus, that would be sold to someone in the community after completion. Students would learn about following blueprints, framing, plumbing, electrical, drywall, roofing, and finish carpentry, which even included cabinet making. I had been to this blind student's home. He wanted me to see his workshop in his garage where he made cabinets. Even though he was blind, he was brilliant, very talented, and wanted to expand his knowledge in the building trades.

A couple of weeks after he enrolled in the class, the instructor came to me in a panic and said, "Oh my God! Your student wants to use power tools and is going to have an accident and seriously hurt himself." I reassured him that he knew what he was doing and had used power tools in his garage. I also reminded him of the laws mandating access to his class. So the student continued to do all the work that the other students did, including the use of power tools. The instructor had to go along with it, but was very concerned.

Near the end of the semester, he came to me again in a panic saying that the guy was working on the roof. I was a little worried this time but didn't let on, as I again reassured him that the student knew his limitations. The student received a good grade and learned how to do carpentry, including how to build a house. So in the end the student was happy, I was happy, and the instructor was relieved, although he did not want any more blind people in his classes.

The student went on to build a church about eight miles from the college. The church was a simple rectangular structure with a steeple and front and back covered porches. What I really thought was funny was that it had no windows. I guess from his perspective, it didn't need any. I understand the windows were added later. He had done a good job on this church. I didn't get to look at the inside, but I'm sure it was all quality work.

Another student, who had broken his back in an automobile accident, enrolled at the college wanting to pursue higher education after he completed his general education and transfer requirements. He was young and very smart. All he really needed was our transportation service. He was married to a very nice young lady and had a couple of kids. He had a great personality and everybody liked and respected him. I had been studying on my own the subject of sexuality and the disabled, which I thought was very interesting. After I built up my nerve, I asked him if he would share with me how he was having children, being paralyzed from the waist down. I explained that I was not being voyeuristic but just trying to educate myself on the subject. He thought about it for a while and answered with a smile, "I'm not going to tell you."

I had been to a conference where one of the workshops covered sexuality. The presentation was put on by a quadriplegic man who only had the use of his neck and head. He was married to an RN who also shared, in detail, their "very fulfilling sex life." You can use your imagination on ways they had sex. He said that even though he was paralyzed from the neck down, he would have orgasms in his mind. Sometimes paralyzed men can even achieve erections even though there's no connection between their brain and penis.

The funny part about the workshop was watching the deaf interpreter's explanation of their activities and body parts. There were a fair number of deaf people at the workshop who seemed very embarrassed by the whole thing. Some of the sign language was so graphic that I too was embarrassed. The paraplegic student of mine who told me that I would never know his secret went on to achieve a higher education, and for years he has been the controller of finances for a city government. Again, he gets the credit for his accomplishments. I just provided the level playing field.

I had another student who was quadriplegic and had only some gross motor movements of his arms. He could not grasp with his fingers, but he could get around by pushing pegs that stuck out on the wheels of his chair. He was from Mississippi and had a deep accent and a great sense of humor. He finished his general education and transfer requirements, went on to become a social worker, and got a job at the state hospital. We became friends and would go to bars to participate in pool tournaments. This man with very little use of his arms and hands could shoot a great game of pool. He once won a tournament at a bar out in the country and made the local paper. He was totally independent and drove his own van with a wheelchair lift and special controls.

I had to be careful not to misunderstand people with heavy Southern accents. I once had a woman in the program talking to me in my office who said her "fillings were really hurting," and she didn't know what to do about it. So I said, "Do you have a dentist where you can go to take care of this?" She said, "No. Why would I want to go to a dentist?" I said, "That's what most people do when their fillings are hurting." She said, "No, you dumb ass, my fillings are hurting." It was then that I realized her feelings were hurt, not her fillings. I was embarrassed.

Another time, she came into my office and wanted to know where she could get some ass. I was shocked, and asked her, "What is it that you want?" She repeated, "I need some ass." It was not uncommon for a male in my position to be approached, so as nicely as I could, I explained that I was a married man and as her counselor I couldn't get involved in that sort of thing. She said, "No, you dumb ass. I want some ass in a cup." I realized then what she really wanted was ice. So I apologized and told her she could find some in the cafeteria. She must've thought I was a real moron for sure, but this time we both had a good laugh.

I had a student who had serious grand mal seizures. When I first met her, my office was next to the school nurse. She had a small corner office with an examination room. The girl was on medication but still had major problems at school a couple of times a week. I asked her what her "aura" was, which is what happens just before a person has a grand mal seizure. She said that just before a seizure she sees death, starts screaming, and then starts into convulsions. She said it had always been a serious problem. She was pretty and smart, and I felt bad for her having this serious problem that she didn't have any control over.

One day I had students waiting inside the office to see me, and the nurse was gone. The administration had located me in the nurse's office, thinking disabled people were a sick group and needed to be near a nurse. Out of the blue this young lady said, "Oh my God! I'm going to have one now." I immediately said, "Let's get in the nurses examination room where you can lie down."

So we both got up, and she raced toward the examination room with me right behind her. She stopped about halfway there, turned around, looked at me, and started screaming in total fear. I grabbed her while she was screaming and pushed her into the examination room. The light was off in the room, and I didn't know where the switch was. She was flailing her arms and slammed the door, shutting us both inside the room. I tried to grab her but wasn't sure where she was. I opened the door to let some light in, and she was on the floor convulsing. So I kept her from hitting her head and turned her head sideways to prevent her from swallowing her tongue.

It looked to the students waiting for me in the office like I was chasing and assaulting this young lady. They ran out in a panic seeking help. It wasn't long before people were coming to her rescue. Her convulsions had stopped, and she appeared uninjured but was extremely exhausted. She rested on a cot while I explained to her rescuers what had happened. We called her parents and when she was feeling better we took her home.

Even though she had this terrible problem she was determined to go to college. The only thing I could do was explain to her instructors that this could happen in class and that they should try to help her instantaneously so she didn't hurt herself. One time she was in the gym talking to the football team just before their practice. I wasn't there, but I heard that she started to have a seizure, screaming and running wildly around in circles. The big football players freaked out and ran from her. Her seizures were a terrible burden, but she was determined to go to school anyway, and God bless her for that. After a couple of semesters she quit coming. I heard a rumor that she had moved and had passed away. I hoped it wasn't true.

I enrolled a new student who had moved from Los Angeles. He was a Vietnam veteran and was suffering from PTSD. He was unkempt and looked very uptight. He explained that he had trouble with anger and rage, depression, and most of the classic symptoms. He seemed anxious and volatile. He said that he wasn't dangerous unless somebody really violated his rights. He told me he had moved from Los Angeles because of his drug background and had once severely injured someone in self-defense over a drug deal gone bad.

I didn't know if he was just crazy and telling me stories, but I knew I would have to watch him for any possible problems. At the time he didn't seem dangerous. His behavior was pretty typical of a lost, crazy, angry, Vietnam vet. I told him that I too struggled with baggage from Vietnam. We talked a long time about his experiences and his goal to turn his life around and get some education. It was the very end of registration, and I would have trouble finding him a full load of twelve units. He said he wanted to attend college so badly that he was willing to take whatever I could give him.

His placement tests indicated that he was lacking in English proficiency and would only be allowed to take remedial courses. I filled his schedule, but the only thing available for English was a class taught by this terrible instructor who failed everybody. I told him I did not want to put him in the class because I knew it would be very upsetting to him to work hard only to receive an F. I warned him about the teacher, but he insisted on taking the class, believing that if he worked hard enough and did well enough, he would surely pass the course. I asked him to keep in touch with me on his progress, because I wanted to be near in case he went into crisis.

I met with this student every day. He told me that this instructor had already warned the class that he would fail everyone who he thought didn't belong in college. He told me that he would work so hard that the instructor would have a change of heart. I felt bad about signing him up for the class knowing that I would be setting him up for failure. He insisted on continuing to stay in the course and take his chances.

At midterm his grade was an F. He came into my office in a total rage and said that he would hurt the man physically if he ended up with an F at the end of the semester. I told him to let me talk to the instructor about the situation and to relax and calm down.

I went to see the instructor at his office and told him that there was a very volatile man in his class who had threatened to hurt him physically if he received an F at the end of the semester even though he was working as hard as he could and completing all of the assignments. I said it was my duty as a counselor to warn him that there could be possible problems if he was treated unfairly.

The English instructor got very angry and said how dare I come into his office to try to intimidate him. I explained again that it was my professional duty to warn him about a student who might become violent if treated unfairly. The instructor was furious and told me that he was not afraid and that I should get the hell out of his office.

At that point I had some options about which I needed to think. One was to drop him from the course against his will, which legally I couldn't do. Another was to call the police and report him for threatening an instructor. I figured the police would talk to him but really wouldn't have enough on him to make an arrest or charge him with anything. If I were to call the police, I would be completely severing my counseling relationship with him because of violating confidentiality and besides, he needed my help to stay grounded. He trusted me, and I didn't want to violate that trust.

My third option was to be there for him when he got the F and work with him during that crisis. I went with the third option and would monitor things while hoping for the best. To make a long story short, everybody in the class failed as usual at the end of the semester except for my student. He received a C.

The student told me, "See. I told you so." He had no idea how much sleep I had lost over him. He went ahead the next semester and took more classes without any problems. He then just disappeared and moved on, and I never heard from him again. I cared about this man. I could feel his intensity, his anger, all of the shit inside of him, and the residue of scars from the war. Like many other combat veterans, he couldn't intellectually understand his feelings. He could only live with them every day.

When I was first hired, my job was to build a program and hire staff. I hired a secretary and enlisted some part-time student aides, but I needed a full-time program assistant because we were getting very busy. I was pretty much free to choose whoever I wanted to fill the position. I advertised in the paper and interviewed several people. One of them was named Nacho. When we first met for the interview, I was taken aback by his looks. He was a burn victim who walked with a bad limp and was extremely disfigured from a terrible automobile accident. Several of his fingers were mere stumps, his arms were badly scarred, and his face could be described as frightening, at least when you saw him for the first time. He had only scar tissue for eyebrows, his nose was just a nub with two holes, and his lips were almost completely gone. His lungs had been burned, and he frequently coughed with a deep rattle. His body from the waist up was engulfed in burn scars.

He told me that he had had numerous operations. I was amazed that someone that badly burned could have survived. He had received some training in accounting at a one-year business school and had been interviewed several times in the community for various positions but never got hired, probably because of his looks.

I interviewed him for a long time. He couldn't help coming across as if this was going to be just another rejection. He avoided eye contact and seemed to be just going through the motions of an interview, knowing he would not get the job. Nacho definitely had the skills that I needed. There was a lot of equipment that needed to be ordered and a transportation program to be developed. Also, I needed someone to help me with the intricacies of writing up a line-item budget for the coming year. How he would relate to the students was an unknown. During the interview there was just something about him that was honest and decent.

I thought about it for a while and decided to hire him. I got the whole thing approved by the vice president, who was my immediate supervisor. I called Nacho to give him the news and to ask him to come in to start the process of being hired. When I saw him he was in a state of shock and couldn't believe that he had finally gotten a job. He told me he would never let me down and got a little choked up. I told him that I didn't hire him because I felt sorry for him, but because he had the skills that I needed in the program and because I knew he would do the job.

Nacho was a real character after his personality started showing. His answer to any question was always "maybe" or "I don't know." Also, he was a great pool player. I must have played him over a hundred games and never won once. Nacho worked for the program for twenty-eight years. He was the best employee that anybody could ever have. He was greatly loved by the disabled students and everybody at the college. He fell in love with a young disabled woman who was a student. She later worked for me as a tutor at the college. They were married, raised a son, and had a great life. He recently died from lung failure that had gotten progressively worse over the years. He was my friend, and I loved him.

After a couple of years, disabled students were a "normal" part of the college milieu. They participated in all of the student activities, hung out in the cafeteria, and were visible all over campus. The disabled student services program had integrated itself and had become a regular part of the college environment. The program office had evolved into a drop-in center for disabled students, their families, and many faculty and staff. Our office was anything but a business-like, stuffy, quiet place where everything is handled by appointment. It was a warm, friendly place, open to all.

It was so different from other offices that constant criticism came from some employees, teachers, and most especially the administrators. They would often drop by with some simple question that could have been handled by a quick phone call. I knew they were really there to see what the hell was going on in this place. As a tenured faculty member, I had the academic freedom to run the place the way I wanted. The real proof in the pudding was that students were succeeding in their classes and many were transferring to four-year colleges and had gotten jobs in the community.

I was often asked to give presentations at the service clubs in town. I was on the local radio station a couple of times, talking about the program. I was also interviewed a couple of times on television. A few times reporters came to the college to take footage to feature the program as part of the news. I provided the local newspaper with articles so the community could see what was going on. This was part of my community awareness program. The more the community knew about the program, the more people with disabilities would want to go to college. The program was generating a lot of dollars because our allocation was based on the number of students.

These allocation funds could only be used within the program, which was mandated by law. While the program was a part of the general student services, the funds were separate, and only I was responsible for them. If there was an audit of my program, I would be held accountable if the funds were not used according to state law. The equipment purchased were things like treadmills and other workout equipment and buses. Of course my policy was to share these machines and equipment with the rest of the campus when they weren't being used by disabled students. The administrators enjoyed that because the college was benefiting from all of this equipment.

One would have thought that I would be highly popular with the administration, but I was not. My PTSD was causing major problems for me. I had problems with authority, and I had major trust issues. It was always my belief that administrators cared much more about their big salaries, power, and suit-and-tie status than for the students. It appeared that the whole college was set up for students, but it is my opinion that it was set up for the few administrators at the top.

Admittedly, I had an attitude that because of my specific area of knowledge I was going to do things my own way. Approaching it this way was a mistake. I did not show the proper respect for the administrators, and they let me know in no uncertain terms that they disliked me. My boss disliked me from the beginning. It came out later that a person who looked just like me had beaten the shit out of him. So, from the start, it was dislike by association. He didn't support me because the president didn't like me, and I think his every wish was to please the president. He knew I could see through him.

I never understood the suits and ties. I guess they tried hard to portray an image of credibility, professionalism, and elitism. I believe that within the administrators' group there existed a pecking order of importance. To me it seemed like they were a very insecure group. I thought that the least important administrator would kiss the ass of the administrator higher up, and that administrator would do the same thing all the way up the line to the president. My

God, if they all kissed ass at the same time it would look like a human daisy chain.

In all fairness, the administrators did get things done. I just disagreed with their priorities, the way they operated, and what I perceived to be a lack of integrity. Through it all I liked to kid them; I'm sure they did the same with me.

During faculty meetings with administrators I spoke freely about what I thought needed to be focused on. Sometimes I would openly disagree with them, which never went over very well. I never felt that it was part of my job to kiss ass or to make administrators feel important. I had no time in my life to play such games. During my career I spent hours in those meetings watching most professors smile and agree when in their hearts I really didn't think they did. I wanted to spend all my time doing the best job I could to meet my professional responsibilities with disabled students. Meetings were a waste of my valuable time.

Each faculty member was required to serve on two or three committees. I had read studies that found that teachers tended to be meek, mild, and responsive to authority. I found that to be fairly accurate. The administration was required by law to organize these committees for the purpose of meeting the legal requirement of something called "shared governance." The faculty along with the administration would decide on total college policy, including the curriculum. These committees actually did not have any authority. The way it worked was that the administration would give the committees things to work on, but all they could really do was make recommendations on issues and policies and give feedback.

I always had a suspicion that they were manipulating the committees to give them what they had already decided on. Occasionally I would point this out along with other truths as to what I thought we were really doing in these meetings, and it would cause major problems. So I was the only faculty member on campus not assigned to committees, with the exception of the Safety Committee, which never met. I also had problems with anger as part of my PTSD and would blow up on administrators in their offices and in meetings. If it were not for tenure and the strong California Teachers Association protecting my rights, I would have certainly been fired several times over, even though I did a great job.

Without strong unions, excellent teachers would lose jobs, be paid inadequate salaries, and receive lousy benefits. Faculty would be reduced to being yes men out of fear of losing their jobs because of personality, personal politics, teaching methods, or anything that didn't fall in line with the values of administrators. The faculty, having no voice in educational decision-making, would give administrators way too much power.

I think that administrators would develop educational policy (how and what to teach) based on their own small set of collective truths, their own political ideologies, and their own religious beliefs. Education, the most important industry in our country, would become biased, stunted, and flawed. Small groups of administrators would control everything and make much bigger salaries than they already did compared to faculty. It was rumored that the chancellor of our college district was actually making more money than the governor of the state. Unions protect staff from unfair personnel practices. Without them administration and faculty relationships would be based on politics and intimidation.

At my college, there existed what was referred to as the "secretarial mafia" (SM), which definitely intimidated faculty, staff, and even administrators. The SM consisted of the older ladies who had worked at the college for a very long time and were in charge of certain departments on campus. They met together often and as a group wielded a lot of power. They were generally mean and strict, and if you crossed one of them you would feel their wrath. They could hold up paperwork on projects and generally take their own sweet time cooperating with you on things that needed to be done right away. If they were against certain changes, chances were they would not get approved or at the very least would be held up. Worst of all, they could and would humiliate you in front of others with no consequences.

So what was the college all about? Was it about the importance of administrators with their expensive clothes and big salaries caught up in their narcissistic little worlds? Was it about faculty caught up in ethnocentricity, teaching truths and knowledge they believed superior to those of other instructors? Was it about the secretarial mafia, the matriarchal guardians of the portal to progress?

No! It was the students. Students were the most important. They were the main focus. They were the life's blood of the college. Without them and the state revenue they generated there would be no college. Students breathed life into the place. They made it interesting, stimulating, and challenging, and it was they who created the college milieu. While there were a few wonderful instructors, most everyone else didn't get it and never really appreciated the students.

I loved the students. I learned from them; they kept me thinking. I couldn't help being swept up in their excitement and creativity. Personally, the students had a positive and therapeutic effect on me. They truly didn't realize what a help they were to me and the baggage I carried from the war. They were what the college was all about, and I will always remember them.

# - 26 -

# HOBO JOHN

My wife, Joanne, and I wanted to start our own community. Joanne was a special education teacher at a nearby grade school, and we both were starting to think about retirement. And so we decided to embark on the great adventure of building an RV park on ten acres located next to a two-lane state highway adjacent to a small, impoverished, agricultural town in the San Joaquin Valley of California. The land was nestled between an orange grove and several hundred acres of hay fields.

When Joanne and I got this idea, we were both about two-thirds through our professional careers. In the beginning we built a small house and planted over seven thousand fast-growing eucalyptus trees. We would drive around until we saw a healthy eucalyptus tree and pick up the seed pods, which contained a bunch of seeds the size of ground pepper. We then germinated them in flats. After the trees were about an inch high they would be transplanted in small paper cups and, when big enough, planted in the ground about three or four feet apart next to a little drip hose. They grew about three feet per month.

During this time we met Hobo John.

For a few days I noticed an older man trying with difficulty to cross the state highway. It was a fifty-five mile per hour two-lane highway; he was obviously having problems seeing the cars and was also hampered by a bad limp as he tried to get across. He was living in the orange grove and was getting water and food from the trash bin at a Mini Mart across the highway. He lived hidden in a corner of the grove, about six rows back from the road, with his spot marked with large empty water bottles.

I decided to find him to see if I could do anything to help. I didn't know what to expect as I approached him. When I greeted him he was in his sleeping bag, dirty. He had a big wooly beard and was surrounded by chicken bones and water bottles. At first he was fearful of me but was soon relaxed, seeing that I posed no threat. He said his name was John Smith, and he told me he had been riding the rails for about forty years as a professional hobo. John was on his way to Texas but had caught the wrong train and had no idea where he was or where to go. He said he was down on his luck, could barely see, and his foot hurt like hell.

We talked for a long time, and I found him to be a verbal, intelligent, and decent person. He was harmless and didn't seem to pose a threat to anyone except himself. I told him not to try to cross the highway; I said I was going to get him some food and water and would be back.

I went home and talked to my wife and six-year-old daughter about John, and they agreed that we should do something to help. They also agreed that we should bring him back to the house and that he could live in an old tent trailer we had on the property. But first I wanted my daughter to meet him to see if she was comfortable about having him move onto our property. She liked him, so we loaded him in the car and brought him home. He smelled so bad that it was necessary to open the car windows.

We set up the trailer in the trees about a hundred feet from the house. He understood that he was welcome to come in and out of our home only when invited and that this arrangement could only work if we had our privacy. I ran a hose out to him for drinking, brushing his teeth, and washing his hands. We gave him a roll of toilet paper and a shovel, so he used the trees to take care of his bathroom needs. We provided some basic bedding and would invite him in the house for meals and to use the shower. He was greatly appreciative and thought he had died and gone to heaven.

I decided to take on the side project of rehabilitating this person. I asked him if he wanted to improve his life, and he seemed eager. I made sure he understood this would be his one and only chance for me to help him get on his feet and that, if he didn't follow through, he would need to move on and could never come back.

First of all I took him to buy some used clothes and some sturdy boots. Having medical problems, I took him to a free clinic. They had free clinics back in those kinder and gentler days for those who had no insurance and no means to pay a doctor. While they were able to correct the bone spur on his foot with injection therapy, they didn't have the equipment to remove the cataracts from his eyes. Having served in the military at one time, he was able to get that fixed through the VA. It took them a long time to find his records with a name like John Smith. Immediately after his surgery I found out that John had enough education that he had learned to read and that he was an avid reader. He read everything he could get his hands on, and he was thrilled to have his eyesight back again. At that time he volunteered to check each dripper on each tree during irrigation time, which was a big help to me. He wanted to earn his keep.

John had lived in serious poverty all his life in some isolated place in the Deep South where he lived with his father and brother. He had interesting stories to tell about how his family hunted for their food and were able to survive. He told me the story about the time he was a young boy and was helping his father chop wood when he accidentally chopped off his big toe. He was driven fifty miles over a dirt road in a A-Model Ford to the nearest doctor. The doctor asked him, "Why didn't you bring the toe?" to which he asked the doctor, "Have you ever tried to get a toe away from twelve hungry chickens?"

I guess times were hard, so he and his brother started the hobo life and never returned home.

As a hobo he had learned all the tricks of survival and subsistence. Survival knowledge and information was passed on by word-of-mouth, such as which houses in particular towns would give out food and where farm jobs were available. Hobos were good at sharing and would often lend each other assistance along the way. They followed the seasons, moving to places that weren't too hot or cold so as to be more comfortable. They usually traveled alone but would meet up with friends at different times around the country. They were like wandering nomads, always traveling and seldom settling down or able to settle down.

When I met John he was on his way to a yearly meeting with his brother in Texas. Traveling was in his blood. It was just the traveling that he liked, not necessarily the destination, although he did tell me about a hobo convention that he and hundreds of other hobos would attend each year somewhere back east. John told me that having your own jar of coffee was respected by the other hobos meaning you were a person with high status.

He said that once after working at some farm he had enough money to buy a new backpack, sleeping bag, and supplies, which of course included a large jar of his own coffee. He tried to catch a moving train, but after he tossed his pack on he realized it was traveling too fast. He was not able to get on, so he just stood there and watched the train with all his earthly belongings disappear into the distance.

He said that hobo life was not a dangerous way to live and that hobos really did not steal that much from each other. They sort of lived off the land, gathering up what food they could along the way to be used for their nightly hobo stew.

I introduced John around the college where everyone called him "Mr. Smith." Everybody liked him and his stories. It so happened that there was an immediate need to keep the leaves off the campus sidewalks because there had been a couple people who had slipped and fallen. I arranged for him to be hired with funds from my program while being supervised through grounds and maintenance. He soon had additional duties and did well. Everybody loved him. I made several attempts to have Mr. Smith talk about his life in a couple of social science classes, but he declined. I also wanted to try to get him on shows like *The Tonight Show Starring*

*Johnny Carson* if I could, because he was fascinating and unique, but he wanted nothing to do with it.

Mr. Smith soon had enough money to rent a small, cheap apartment with a kitchenette that was close to the college. I was hoping that he could apply for the next opening in maintenance where the position would be full-time with medical benefits. He would have the money to buy a car and become a fully independent citizen. What a grand opportunity and one that he could achieve through his own hard work.

To everyone's disappointment Mr. Smith started missing work and started drinking. I would talk to him about it, and he just kept telling me that he could hear that train whistle blowing. He was growing increasingly unhappy and ended up getting fired. He was seen sleeping in a field in a cardboard refrigerator box and then sleeping under a bridge. Then he just disappeared and went back to being Hobo John.

Wow! What lessons we can learn from this, and what information we can extrapolate from it:

1.  On a small scale it was a lot more difficult to change Hobo John's culture and values than I thought it would be.
2.  On a larger scale, and aside from the main story, and to make a point, maybe losing precious American lives and pouring money into trying to change the Middle East theocracies into free American democracies, and trying to change their culture and values into our American culture and values is futile and wrong. As with John, trying to change peoples' cultures does not work.

# - 27 -

# THE RV PARK

After twelve years we cut the trees down, sold them for firewood, and began construction of the RV park. We knew we would have people living there semi-permanently who were extremely poor. Residing in small trailers is a way for people living in poverty to have shelter and survive very inexpensively.

We were hoping most of our customers would be overnight RVs traveling down the highway. It didn't exactly turn out that way. Most of our clientele turned out to be dirt poor. They lived off of state disability checks, welfare, Social Security disability, and some had menial jobs.

We both wanted this park to be a good place to live, with a laundry room, clean bathrooms, and pristine landscaping. We wanted people to keep their individual spaces clean and free of trash. We wanted a safe place for all to live, with no crime and no drugs. We wanted people to get along, to be decent and respectful to one another, and to take pride in this community.

The long-timers lived in the back section of the RV park, where it was quieter and provided more privacy, while the front was reserved for people travelling through. We could see that there was a huge socioeconomic gap between the short-timers who traveled in expensive, state-of-the-art motor homes and fifth wheels and the resident poor who lived permanently in shabby little trailers. The residents jokingly called the front "Beverly Hills" and the back "Beverly Hillbillies." We wanted them somehow to be able to coexist in peace and harmony.

Managing the poverty element would turn out to be a challenging endeavor, given the fact that along with poverty comes a whole array of social problems: health problems, drug and alcohol addiction, poor nutrition, psychological issues, and more. It was our experience that people living in poverty tended to be under-educated, many unable to read, and limited in communication skills.

This is not to say that all poor people are this way. We had plenty of residents who were honest, loving, smart, and decent, who were just down on their luck. They were perhaps victims imprisoned in the culture of poverty and ignorance. Some were in poor health, while others lacked the opportunity to improve their lives because of making bad decisions. No matter what their background, it was our challenge to develop this community, to establish norms for living, and to come up with community rules by which everyone could abide.

We wanted a place where people would have a sense of community, living safely and peacefully, feeling good about themselves, and being good neighbors to one another.

As it turned out, we think that we accomplished most of the above. I wore many different hats to make this happen: small town sheriff, preacher, counselor, animal control guy, manager, judge, jury, and friend. We had to utilize every bit of our educational training and experience, relying heavily on our counseling and organizational skills. For this to work, we needed to respect and connect with people and to lead by example. As part of our formula for success, we also had to include a lot of humor.

My perspective should in no way be interpreted as prejudicial, mean-spirited, or degrading of others who are less fortunate than I. I will tell the story of our experiences, which were funny, loving, interesting, and sometimes sad. I will talk about relationships, individual dramas, and other stories about life in our park. The events I will later relate to, focus more on the poor residents who lived there permanently than on the over-nighters and snowbirds who followed the seasons. But first I will breeze over the birth of the RV park.

# - 28 -

# BUILDING THE RV PARK

After formulating our ideas about how we wanted the park to look, we went to the county with our written plans and drawings. We had to prove that our RV park would have a positive impact socially, economically, and aesthetically, and we had to demonstrate how it would benefit the surrounding area. We were also required to have an environmental impact report to show what effect the sewage would have and whether there were any kit foxes living there. Included in the report was a survey to find whether there was evidence of Native American habitation of archaeological significance.

After the general plans were approved by the county, we went to the bank. I sat at various times by the highway, counting the actual RVs that passed by. We told the bank that we were the RV Park that travelers would get to first after traveling about fifty miles from a large town headed north toward many of the recreational areas in the Sierra Nevada. We also had to prove to the bank that we could make payments based on an extrapolation of what income we could make. Based on all of this information, and after what seemed to me an eternity, the bank approved the project, and the construction began!

We had to grade the property to form the right drainage and cut the individual trailer spaces, which had to be level. The next step was building a bathhouse and a laundry room. It had a women's bathroom and shower on one end, a men's bathroom and shower on the other, a laundry room in the middle, and a small office. We had to do most of the work, which consisted of hundreds of feet of trenching. In RV parks, most of the work is underground.

I figured that I could rent a backhoe and do the trenching myself, saving thousands of dollars. When the trencher arrived, the delivery person showed me the basic operation of this machine. It had six levers on the top and two foot pedals on the bottom. I did hire a general contractor to help us build the park, and so most of the building would be done by just him and me.

With the trenching, we had to start with a three-and-a-half-foot deep ditch for sewage and dig at a one to three percent grade that would end up at the huge septic tank at the rear of the property. The ditch would be seven-feet deep where it connected to the septic tank. It had to be a gradual slope so the excrement and toilet paper would float their way to destiny. Two years later, when we pumped the tank for the first time, we found a few beer bottles and cans, a couple of shoes, many diapers, and a lot of female sanitary napkins in addition to the excrement.

The first three days of me operating the backhoe proved to be extremely dangerous for anyone standing nearby. I was so frustrated trying to learn, I spent three nights in my sleep operating levers and pedals. It was driving me crazy. After three days, the light bulb finally came on in my head, and I was ready to do a proper job of it.

After the trenching was done, with the sewer pipe connecting all the spaces to the septic tank, it was time for the big test. I poured about ten gallons of water down the sewer pipe at space number one, ran to the septic tank at the back of the property, opened the lid, and waited to see the water drain into it. I waited there, watching and hoping for over an hour, and saw nothing. It got dark and I went into the house feeling depressed, thinking that I would have to redo the whole thing to correct the problem. In the morning I walked back to the septic tank and looked again. This time I saw about a ten gallon puddle in the tank. It just took longer to meander its way to the tank than I had expected. Hallelujah!

We then installed all the water lines leading from our well to the various spaces, laundry room, and irrigation locations. We ran all the gopher-proof, direct burial electric cables and phone lines. After all of this was in place, and during every other phase of the construction for that matter, we had to meet with the building inspector's approval, which was always nerve-racking.

One dangerous mishap occurred one afternoon when I was working alone. I was connecting twelve thirty-feet deep dry wells, four feet in diameter, lined with brick and topped with a concrete cap. I was trenching around the dry wells, connecting them to each other, when I stepped out of the backhoe to measure the depth of the trench and fell backwards into the dry well. I fell seven feet and landed on my side on the concrete cap.

So there I was in a deep hole with blood streaming down my face. I thought at first that my neck was broken. I moved slowly and was reassured to find that my neck was okay, but I could not get to my feet. The pain was intense from a separated shoulder and a banged-up knee. I had been through a war and never got this injured. It was early August, and the temperature was over one hundred degrees. In the hole itself it felt ten degrees hotter. I realized I was in shock, and every time I tried to get to my feet I would black out. My kids and my wife thought I was on the tractor because they could hear it running. I knew that if I could not get out of there I would probably die.

Finally I was able to get on my feet. I reached up with my one good arm, grabbed hold of the tractor step, and was able after several tries to throw my good leg out of the hole and roll myself out. I lay there for awhile until I was able to climb back up on the tractor and drive myself to the front door. Of course my family was shocked and drove me to the emergency room. No surgery was necessary as my shoulder would eventually come back together on its own, and I knew that with a sling I could continue to work, returning to the backhoe to finish on time.

# - 29 -

# GRAND OPENING

In the next couple of weeks the work was completed, and the entrance sign was up. We were ready for our grand opening. This was a happy time for us, until we realized nobody was driving in. After about five days we knew we were in trouble. We were going to have to get busy quickly to make payments to the bank.

The next day, a carnival worker showed up from about a half a mile away where he and his troupe were camping at a storage yard. He asked if the carnies could move to the RV park and live in their trailers. The county had notified them that they could not live at the storage yard where they kept the amusement rides. Of course we said, "Sure! Come on down!"

About half a dozen ratty-looking trailers showed up and paid us a month in advance. Half of them had families who all appeared to work in some capacity for the carnival. They were all grimy with grease stains on their clothing, and I noticed that the adults had terrible dental problems. One of them, Tommy, informed me that he had just removed an abscessed tooth with a pair of pliers. The adults were missing several teeth and did not look healthy to me.

The plan was that they would leave their trailers at the RV park when they were on the road and would sleep beneath their rides or in a small crowded bunk trailer provided by the carnival for twenty-five dollars per week. At first I felt sorry for them, suspecting they were being exploited by the carnival owner, but they were proud of their jobs and seemed to possess a strong work ethic. They didn't seem to mind or question the long hours for very little pay. They were obviously uneducated and seemed to gravitate toward dirty jobs that were available to them. They all had a background of drugs and arrests and said they had all moved here from Oklahoma.

At first I was worried about having them live at the park. After I got to know them, though, I realized that they were happy for the most part and seemed to be decent people. I informed them of the RV park rules. There could be no drugs, no loud noise at night, and no stealing or vandalism. I tried to bond with these people, and eventually I was able to forge some good relationships. They understood that the minute they were paid, they had to pay the rent and electricity before they went to the nearby casino in the mountains where they won their fortunes. They spoke with Southern accents and completely destroyed the English language. One of the men would end each of his sentences with "and stuff 'n all." They all smoked and drank beer. There were no domestic problems nor did they exhibit any violence toward one another. I enjoyed drinking an occasional beer with them and found their stories of carnival life fascinating.

Part of their diet was fresh mustard greens picked from a part of the property that was not developed yet. They told me how to pick the greens and how to cook them. All my life I had considered these to be nothing but weeds with little yellow flowers growing alongside the roads and in fields. I had never considered eating them. So my wife and I started picking these leaves and sautéing them with a little oil and vinegar. They turned out to be very healthy and delicious, and, of course, free.

The carnie people would also fish for catfish in the nearby irrigation canals. They knew just where to go and would return with a large catfish or two most of the time. One of them said that the first time he saw a catfish's face he jumped back in horror because it looked just like his ex-wife. These people were real characters and possessed their own unique brand of humor.

One family had so much clutter around their trailer that I had to loan them my rake and constantly remind them to keep the place clean. I explained that other new people coming in would see a mess and probably turn around and drive back out. I realized that I couldn't break them completely of their lifelong habit of throwing everything on the ground, but as long as they raked their area frequently I was willing to compromise. Another resident, Mike, would reach out the window of his trailer with a bag of trash and flip it up on the top of his roof. I first noticed about half a dozen bags of trash on top of his trailer and had to talk to him about never doing that again as the dumpster was just a short distance away.

In time, more trailers started to dribble in, having heard about us from other RV parks in the area. I guess the word got out from a kind of trailer trash network of communication.

I had to turn away many of them because I sensed major problems. One man showed up with a small, fairly decent-looking trailer. He had alcohol on his breath and had rheumy eyes. I told him I was sorry, but I didn't think it would work out with him living there.

He begged me to give him a try for a day or two so he could prove to me that he would be just fine. He said he had traveled a long distance and was hired at a nearby nut-processing factory as a welder in the maintenance department. I relented and told him I would try him out for a couple of days. Late that same night, some women came to our trailer complaining that he was really bothering them and that he was totally drunk. I walked over to talk to him only to find him passed out in the middle of the road between the trailer rows. I shook him and told him to get up before he got run over. He replied, "Go screw yourself. I'm sleeping right here tonight." I told him I would get the police to get him up and have him thrown in jail. He immediately agreed to move.

I helped him up and half-carried him to his trailer. I laid him on the picnic table by his trailer so I could open his door and push him inside. When I opened his door, I found that the trailer was packed to the roof with his belongings, and there was no way to get inside. The next morning I went to his picnic table and told him to get the hell out of the park and that his trial period had been short-lived. He obliged.

Another family had a six-year-old boy. I thought they made a decent first impression and so I let them move in. They requested to park their trailer at the far corner nearest the highway. A few days later I noticed several big rigs parked on the frontage road in front of the park. I also noticed other truck drivers coming to their trailer every fifteen minutes. It turned out that the father had a CB radio and was soliciting truck drivers passing by the highway for sex with his wife. Their business was prostitution. When I kicked them out and threatened to call the police, I asked the lady, "How can you do that kind of work in front of your husband and your son?" She replied, "I like it."

Most of the people we kicked out would go willingly. A couple of them told me that they knew their rights and knew that I couldn't kick them out for months and that they would not pay the rent during that time. All I had to say to them, which worked every time, was, "Do you see this hundred dollar bill? It's yours the second you drive out of the exit with your trailer." They were more than happy to get the bill, and we were happy to cut our losses.

We started seriously wondering what in the world we had gotten ourselves into with this business; it seemed the bottom rung of society was constantly knocking at our door. We realized later that better days were ahead when many fine people started to move in. They would tell us that they had driven by before and didn't even see us off the highway.

It was Joanne's idea to order fourteen international flags and place them in front of our park on poles. Her thinking was that the movement of the flags would catch the attention of those passing by on the highway, which is exactly what happened. Shortly after that, our park was full and we were more than able to make the monthly payments to the bank.

Our park was full of all kinds of people. Besides the carnival workers, we had disabled people who lived on their Social Security and state disability checks. We had overnighters who were retired professionals with upscale trailers and motor homes. There were vacationers, retired "Snowbirds" who traveled the seasons, and even a few professional people who worked nearby and had chosen to live in a trailer to cut expenses.

Interestingly, all of these people got along. They were all adhering to the park rules and the established norms which included waving to one another, being considerate, keeping the bathrooms clean, and showing simple respect for one another. This was not to say we didn't have problems that necessitated me wearing my law enforcement hat. If kids screwed up, I would take their bicycle privileges away for a few days. I got along very well with the kids in the park, and they didn't seem to mind if I provided a little structure for them. In fact, they responded positively to it.

There was a couple I placed in the back who caused trouble. The guy was a hard-core alcoholic and was not good to his wife. She was one of the sweetest people I have ever met. I asked her once why she didn't leave him, and she replied that she had nowhere to go. She was dependent on him to support her. He was a retired well-digger who was making a decent amount of money through his own business.

One time I caught him driving around the park completely inebriated. I told him to park the car where it was and go back to his trailer. I explained that we had kids playing around the park and that I could not allow him to drive around drunk. He went back to his trailer and had his wife drive the car back to his space. The next morning I told him that I was suspending his driving privileges within the park and said I would have him arrested if I ever caught him driving drunk again.

He didn't drive in the park for a couple of months, and word got back to me that he was complaining that I had taken away his license. He must have believed that I had the authority to do that, as if I were the Department of Motor Vehicles or something. After a couple of months I told him he could drive again in the park, but he would have to be sober.

Another time I received complaints that he was walking around outside of his trailer naked. I went over to talk to him to find him with his door open, lying nude on the couch. I again threatened him; he suggested that I go to hell and told me that I couldn't tell him what to do inside of his trailer. The next day he apologized and said he wouldn't do that again. I had come close numerous times to kicking him out of the park, but his sweet wife, who was getting lots of support from her neighbors, prevented me from doing that. For her sake, I just put up with the guy.

# - 30 -

# SOCIALIZATION

Every couple of months we held a potluck under a large canopy in front of our motor home. This helped to keep the whole community together. People were friendly and accepting of the differences in each other. Differences in socioeconomic status between the people in front with their nice RVs and the people in the back with their not-so-nice trailers were quite apparent, including the way they used language to express themselves. In general the cultural differences were profound, yet people got along well and had a lot of fun.

I observed that the lines between the lower class, the middle class, and sometimes the upper middle class were at times blurry. The higher class people often took a liking to the lower class people and would sometimes discuss them with me saying things like, "I met so-and-so and they were very nice. Is there anything I can do for them?"

In my lifetime I have lived in many neighborhoods where people disliked their neighbors or had never met them at all. We do have a class system in this country, and it hasn't been my experience that people cross over that often and assimilate that easily. The interaction in our RV park, even though on a small scale, was both surprising and fascinating to me. The difference between our park and a regular community I think had to do with size and the fact that the middle class people in the front were only there a short time compared with the people in the back.

At our picnics I would usually provide the hamburgers, hotdogs, and pop, and others would bring the salads and desserts and whatever else they wanted to drink. Being an old sociology man, I was particularly interested in all of the blended interactions I observed. During these occasions, I would provide an invitation to the new people in the front to join the celebrations, and most of the time they would accept. I would introduce them, brag a little about them, and try to make them feel comfortable and accepted, which they always were. For the most part, they wouldn't stay at the party as long as the people in the back, but they seemed to enjoy themselves.

To be perfectly honest, I was a little hesitant to eat the salads and desserts, knowing that some of the people were hygiene-challenged. I always had a good excuse not to eat some of the food, and I tried not to hurt anybody's feelings. These potluck celebrations were a bit intense at the end because people wanted to claim the empty cans and would sometimes fight over them. Most of the people collected and saved empty cans to supplement their incomes. These get-togethers, at least for the people in the back, provided them with a sense of community, which they seemed proud to be a part of and that they had probably never experienced before.

Music was always a part of our social gatherings. Our kindly neighbor Pete, who lived in a trailer next to our motor home, had a couple of guitars, a microphone and speakers. He was a widower in his eighties who had tragically lost his family. He was alone except for some close friends who also had a trailer in our park. He loved country music and would often play with friends at a local bar just for the fun of playing. He always looked forward to our barbeques and would take great pleasure in providing some entertainment for us.

One time a friend of my wife came over with copies of lyrics she had printed out. She planned on playing her guitar and leading others in song. Surprisingly, no one wanted to sing, with several using the excuse that they didn't have their glasses with them. We were saddened to finally figure out what the real problem was: most of them couldn't read the words.

Twice each month a lady and her husband in the back would provide karaoke. Linda and Sam were in their early sixties and had been married forever. They had family who would visit frequently, especially during the karaoke events. Linda and Sam never really got along. Whenever she would try to solicit his help for something, he would always respond, "It ain't my job." She would look disgusted, but I think she secretly loved him and he did her.

Linda had acquired a karaoke machine somewhere along the line. One of her favorite things to do was to offer her karaoke services to whoever wanted them. She would do karaoke at a nearby beer tavern on a weekly basis. She had a few singers (karaoke groupies) who would show up wherever she was doing karaoke. They were nice people, but they didn't seem to be able to sing very well; in fact, none of them could carry a tune.

At the get-togethers at the RV park, you didn't have to be an expert in music to know that the singing sounded like a bunch of sick dogs. Not singing well was inconsequential, though. I think they really believed they were singing beautifully. Linda, who directed it all, would sometimes say into the microphone, "Okay y'all. This one is going out to Bill and Joanne." We couldn't help but feel honored for the dedication. When the party was over, she would ask her husband to help carry the equipment back to the trailer. He would respond, "It ain't my job." Then a few people would fight over who was getting the empty cans, and they would all go back to their trailers.

# - 31 -

# THE BIG WEDDING

Jake and Marie lived in a fifth wheel in the middle part of the park. Jake was one of the nicest people in the park, but he was a serious alcoholic. He worked at the saw mill a few miles up the highway on the maintenance crew, which was a difficult and dangerous job. When he wasn't doing that, he did welding for a couple of different companies in the area. Every night when he got home from work, he would hit the alcohol and eat the dinner that Marie had prepared for him.

Marie would also deliver dinner to a man who lived at the very end of the park. He was a burned-out, former drug addict who rarely left his trailer. He was also a very nice man who never caused any problems. He claimed to have been in a rock band years ago and got involved in using heavy drugs that ruined his career. His name was Larry, and he looked just like Charlie Manson without the swastika on his forehead. Larry got the nickname "San Quentin Larry" because he stayed in his trailer about twenty-three hours a day. He was a nice man, peaceful and interesting, who lived on state disability.

Marie, a burned-out former drug addict herself, was friendly and loving toward everybody in our park. Marie and Jake were living together and both had adult children from former marriages who would visit on the weekends and have barbecues where everyone would get drunk. But they always paid the rent and never caused any problems. Marie just seemed to love everybody. Both Joanne and I liked these people.

For years Marie had been pressing Jake to marry her. Jake, who liked life just the way it was, was never ready to make that commitment. People would ask Marie why she was willing to marry a man who had a tremendous alcohol problem. She would say that at least she knew exactly what she was getting. One day Marie wore him down on the subject and he agreed. She was so happy that she was telling everybody in the park about their plans. Joanne and I didn't take the whole thing very seriously, but we told them that we were happy for them.

Marie came to me, asked if I would marry them, and wanted to know if they could have the wedding in the RV park on a patch of grass right next to the bathrooms. I explained that I was sorry, but I couldn't marry anybody because I didn't have a license to do so and that the marriage would not be legal or legitimate. Marie said they didn't care if it was legal. She said that if they could just go through a ceremony with everybody in the park in attendance then she would consider it a real marriage regardless of the legalities.

I was happy to let them have their ceremony in the park, but I told them that I didn't feel comfortable officiating; however, I knew somebody who might. Her name was Dr.

Hadley, a preacher who had her own church in a small town about twenty miles away. The church happened to be a place where a lot of the recovering alcoholics and drug addicts went to worship. Marie knew Dr. Hadley and thought it was a wonderful idea. Dr. Hadley agreed to do the ceremony even though she could not grant them a marriage license. As I remember, it had something to do with either a Social Security problem or the fact that one of them had never gotten a legal divorce from their last marriage.

Marie and Jake and all their relatives and friends at the park were overjoyed. All the plans and preparations were underway, and the wedding was a go!

Joanne and I committed ourselves to providing picnic tables borrowed from the spaces and doing what we could to support the event. The wedding reception was to be a potluck affair, and Joanne would provide the soft drinks. Jake would rent a tuxedo, and Marie would borrow a beautiful white wedding dress. There would be a best man and a maid of honor along with several bridesmaids and flower girls.

The day of the wedding everything was in place, and there were approximately seventy-five people who would attend. The plan was for the wedding procession to emerge from the women's bathroom and walk to the awaiting groom and Dr. Hadley, who would perform the ceremony. The laundry room, located right next to the bathroom, would be used to keep the cake and the food for the reception. It would be neatly laid out and served from the long laundry folding table next to the washers and dryers.

At the last minute, the karaoke woman realized that there was no wedding march music. She ran to her trailer and produced the perfect song for the occasion. The bathroom door swung open and out came the wedding procession with the song, "Stand by Your Man" blaring. The groom was waiting and was so drunk he was having difficulty standing up. "Stand by Your Man" was more like "Hold Up Your Man." The ceremony was, in its own right, serious and traditional; there wasn't a dry eye to be found. This was truly the hokiest, most ridiculous wedding I have ever been to, but I was a little choked up myself. I knew how important it was to Marie, and I think Jake was happy, too, although he appeared to be so drunk that he didn't know exactly what was going on.

There was no PA system, so nobody could hear the words that were being spoken or the exchange of vows, but I'm sure they were beautiful. After the bride and groom kissed and were introduced as Mr. and Mrs., the people attending gave them a roar of applause with whooping and hollering. The line then started to form at the laundry room door for the food and refreshments. The picnic tables were covered with party paper, including small ornaments in the middle. People ate, drank, and joyfully shared in this occasion.

Jake could not stay very long because he was so drunk he had to go back to his trailer. Marie, however, stayed for the whole celebration. Everybody had contributed plenty of alcohol for the occasion, and the bash was on.

Joanne and I stayed and joined in the celebration for about an hour and then went back to our motor home. The party went on for hours. I heard later that it got pretty wild, and it was not without problems. The next day I was told that Gay George and Carnie Joe had a bet going to see who had the longest "dally wacker." They unzipped their pants and leaned at the end of a table where they displayed their private parts for measuring. The problem was that three of Marie's female friends were sitting at that same table. The women were so furious at this display of disrespect by the two men that they physically attacked them. Other people quickly broke up the fight, and the two men were ordered to leave the party.

I had organized a volunteer crew to clean up after the party. During the cleanup time, a man, who claimed the cans were his, actually got so angry that he drove his car up on the lawn by the picnic tables as if he were going to run people over to get them. The next day, after my investigation, he maintained that he was only trying to intimidate the other people who wanted the cans and to get them to back off.

Folks called him the "Bee Man" because he had his own bee-keeping business producing honey for sale. I think he was the most disliked, unpopular person in the park. Other than that incident, he never caused any problems, stayed to himself, and always paid his rent on time. He just had a terrible personality, was dirty, and smelled bad all the time. Each day he managed to corner me for twenty minutes and parrot a popular conservative radio host as if this man were actually expounding on ideas of his own. Other than that he was okay, and I forgave him for the incident.

The two men who were measuring their private parts swore up and down that they didn't remember doing any of that and couldn't apologize enough. Thinking back on it, I think the alcoholic blackout they claimed to have had was a convenient excuse that they had probably used many times in their lives. At a "normal" wedding reception, it would have been unbelievably repulsive. I am sure it would have ruined the whole wedding, and it would have left lasting memories of total disrespect for the bride and groom. The people involved would have surely gone to jail.

At this wedding however, it was no big deal. People didn't seem to mind, and, in fact, they were laughing about it later on. The three women at the table who were furious when it first happened seemed to quickly get over it. It was interesting to me that the social norms I was observing in this community were markedly different from the general moral values of American society. When these kinds of things happened they were short-lived, and people were never really that surprised.

# - 32 -

# OBESITY IN THE RV PARK

I n the park people were either skinny or really fat; there were not many in between. I don't know whether this phenomenon was because of bad nutrition, too much of the wrong foods, or both. A man and woman came to the park driving an old van and pulling a small trailer. They were really nice people, and I couldn't help but notice that the gentleman was morbidly obese. I would estimate that he weighed between five and six hundred pounds. He sat in the passenger seat while his wife drove. When their van pulled into the driveway it was leaning over to one side. His wife did all the work unhooking the trailer while he stayed in the van.

I felt very sad for him and wondered how anyone could get that overweight. He spent most of the time sitting in the van I guess because it was more comfortable than the trailer. I felt bad for him realizing that he had imprisoned himself in this huge body, and I knew he was probably extremely uncomfortable. The only time he would get out of the van was to use the bathroom in his trailer. He would then return to the van under great physical strain.

This man was severely physically limited because of his weight. About three days after they moved in he had a heart attack. The ambulance showed up but had to call for reinforcements because two people could not lift him onto the stretcher. Two more ambulances showed up, and it ended up taking six people to lift him into the ambulance. A few hours later his wife came back to the park only to hook up the trailer and pull out. I was not there at the time to give her a refund or to find out her husband's condition. I don't know whether she picked him up from the hospital to move on or just what happened to him as I didn't know to which hospital the ambulance had taken him. I couldn't help but to assume the worst.

There was a young carnival worker and his wife who had lived there for a few months. They were both about nineteen years old. He was physically strong, and she was extremely overweight. I would hire this young man once or twice a week to help me around the park. One time while we were doing a job, we walked past his trailer. His wife, dressed in a bikini, was sunbathing on a blanket between the spaces. When I looked at her I was shocked that a woman of her size would wear a bikini. As we walked by I looked away as if I didn't see her, and of course I kept my observations to myself. Her husband on the other hand looked at her and said in all seriousness, "How is a man supposed to get any work done?" I guess beauty truly is in the eye of the beholder.

There was a family with two children who wanted to move in. The younger boy was seven and the other was a teenager. When I asked what kind of income they had, he convinced me that he was working a full-time job. He and the kids took care of his wife, who was extremely heavy. I estimated that she must have weighed about four hundred and fifty pounds. To get her in and out through the trailer door, they had to push and shove for a long time to squeeze her through, so she spent most of the time, if not all, in the trailer. The father and the two kids were very protective of her and took good care of her.

About a week after they moved in, a sheriff's deputy pulled in, put handcuffs on the father, and took him away. That left the teenager and his brother to care for their mother. Being in jail caused him to lose his job, and nobody knew exactly what he had done or when he was going to get out. So the family essentially had no income at that point. They had paid a month's rent in advance and told me that they had plenty of food. That gave me some time to figure out what I was going to do about their situation.

People started complaining that the laundry room smelled really bad. I looked in the trash can to try to find the problem and found feces wrapped in newspaper. I didn't know who had done this, and it continued to happen every day. I finally figured out that the woman was unable to use the toilet in the trailer, or it didn't work. She was going to the bathroom on newspaper and having one of the kids take it to the laundry room for disposal in the trashcan. I instructed them to put her waste in the large trash bin away from the other trailers.

Once a week the kids would squeeze her out the door and load her in the car. They would drive her up on the lawn next to the entrance of the women's bathroom so that she could take a shower. After she showered, her kids would put her back in the car, take her to the trailer, and inch by inch push her through the door.

Every time she showered, she would leave behind a terrible odor in the shower stall. She was so big that she apparently could not use the toilet. It was my guess that once she sat on the toilet she was unable to stand up again. She was evidently defecating and urinating in the shower and then squishing the solid part through the drain grid to wash it down the shower drain. It was causing a huge problem in the bathroom that seemed to linger for days.

I realized finally that I could not tolerate this any longer and that they would have to move out. I talked to them about it as gently and respectfully as I could. I explained that she needed more assistance than the RV park could give her. I offered to give them a one hundred dollar bill when I saw them driving out. She had found another place to live, I think with her sister, so I didn't feel that bad about insisting that they go. I often wonder if she's still alive.

# - 33 -

# THE SHOWERHEAD MYSTERY

On a daily basis residents were coming to me complaining that there was no showerhead in the women's bathroom, so I was making numerous trips to the hardware store to buy more showerheads. At first I thought some kid was behind it, but I didn't know who it might be. Every day a shower head would continue to disappear. I ended up buying each woman in the park her own personal showerhead.

I began to notice that a particular woman who lived alone was coming to us repeatedly complaining that the showerhead was missing. She would knock on the door and tell me, "Well, they did it again!" and then watch for my reaction. I figured that she must be the one taking the showerheads and decided to search around her trailer. She lived in the back in a space by a dirt bank and some eucalyptus trees.

When I looked over the bank in back of her trailer I discovered a bunch of showerheads that had been thrown over. I still have no idea why she did this. Possibly it gave her a sense of control or satisfied some other weird need.

When I confronted her, she admitted stealing the showerheads and said she didn't know why she did it. I told her, "Do you see this brand-new hundred dollar bill? It's yours when I see you driving out the entrance."

# - 34 -

# THE HORSE STORY

A s I mentioned, our park was located in a rural area. Everything was going well, but I suppose there were periods of boredom for some of the residents, especially the kids. I wondered what I could do to provide a better place, a little more stimulation perhaps. I was talking to my friend Henry, who had been one of my students at the college. He had recently become a schoolteacher, and his wife worked at the college. They were both good people, and we had become friends over the years. They previously lived in Oklahoma but decided to move to California close to where their adult children lived. I think that they also needed a little more stimulation in their lives, hence the impetus for making the move from Oklahoma.

Henry was a real character and a storyteller. He talked slowly with a deep drawl and had a lot of funny stories to tell about Oklahoma. One of the stories was about being in a very conservative Southern Baptist church where he was waiting to witness a double baptism of two older ladies. In the front of the church by the altar was a baptismal font where the ceremony would take place. Adjacent to the font there was a partition where the ladies would change their clothes in preparation to go into the water.

Just at the wrong time while they were changing, the partition completely fell over to expose the two naked ladies. When it happened there was dead silence in the church except for some rustling around and people looking down—not to mention the ladies desperately trying to cover themselves. People ran up to erect the partition, but the harm had already been done. Henry said there was a momentary denial of what had happened, but after that people slowly started to chuckle.

Another story that he told was about a couple of farmers trying to get rid of a very old culvert-like cement structure at the end of town. All the farmers in the area brought their tractors to try to remove it. They tried and tried, to no avail. The cement thing was too strong and too heavy, so they decided to blow it out with dynamite.

They dug many holes and placed the dynamite in just the right places and got ready for the explosion. They had put out a warning to the town that at a certain time they were going to blow this thing up. The time came and the dynamite was ignited. When the dust cleared the cement structure was still there intact, but most of the windows in town were broken. So what turned out to be a project of the removal of the concrete turned out to be the farmer's project of paying for and replacing all the broken windows in town.

Henry and I were talking one day about a horse that he had just acquired. He said he was driving by a field when he noticed the horse that was emaciated; it was literally skin and bones. Henry loved animals and was so disturbed seeing this starving horse that he rented a horse trailer and a pair of wire cutters and returned to the field. He cut through the fence and began to load the horse onto the trailer.

Just then, the owner drove up and said, "What in the hell are you doing with that horse? That horse belongs to me." Henry told him in simple words, "Not anymore!" He told the man that if he gave him a hard time he would call the authorities and show them what he had done to this animal. The man finally relented, and Henry drove off with the horse.

Henry lived on five acres and had a perfect place to keep it. After a couple of months he had nursed it back to health and had become very attached. He loved that horse, which, judging by its teeth, he figured was about seventeen years old. His grandkids could actually play safely under and around its legs. Despite the abuse it had suffered, it was a gentle animal and became part of the family.

About a year later, Henry's wife put a lot of pressure on him to move into town, closer to the college. He was talking to me about boarding the horse somewhere and asked if I knew of a place. I thought that the horse would be just what the park needed, so I invited him to build a corral and board the horse at the trailer park. So Henry and I built a temporary corral until we could build a much bigger area for it beside the trailers.

Henry agreed to keep the horse fed and watered, and the next day brought it over and put it in the corral, which attracted a lot of attention. The kids were excited, petted its nose and fed it carrots. Everybody seemed excited, and I was pleased because I thought the horse gave the trailer park a nice touch of country.

The next morning I noticed the horse lying down. As I got closer to it, I realized it had died during the night. I knew I had to call Henry right away, which I dreaded. The people in the park were shocked and saddened. At that point I realized that the horse was no longer a nice attraction. When I broke the news to Henry, he wept and said he would be right over.

When he got there he looked at the horse and cried; he really loved that horse. After he got control of himself, he asked, "What are we going to do now?" Consoling him, I said I would make some calls to see what to do with the carcass. There were some dairies within a radius of about twenty miles. I figured cattle would die occasionally, and they would know what to do. I called the dairy and they said that there was a company that picked up large dead animals. I called the company and asked when they could pick up the horse. They told me it would take two or three weeks before they could do the job.

I couldn't leave a dead horse lying around for that long, so I asked Henry if we could just rent a backhoe and bury it right in the field. He agreed that this would be the best thing to do. I drove to the rental yard with my truck and picked up a medium-sized backhoe. The plan was to dig a trench wide enough and deep enough for the horse to fit and then push it in with the blade on the back of the backhoe. I told Henry that it was okay to go home and that I had the situation handled, but Henry felt he needed to stay to wish the horse a personal farewell.

I started digging a trench a little more than the length of the horse. Everything was going well until I hit hardpan about six and a half feet down. It was so hard at that depth that I just couldn't go any farther. I then drove around and, using the blade of the backhoe, slowly pushed the horse near the trench. I wanted the feet and legs to drop in first followed by the body. I slipped the horse gently into the trench but rigor mortis had set in and the horse was standing up in the ditch with his head sticking out.

Henry said, "Hell, Bill, we can't bury him like that because the coyotes will get him." I thought about it for a while, sitting on the backhoe, looking at this horse standing upright in the ditch with his head sticking out. I told Henry that I would have to mash it down into the hole with the power of the backhoe hydraulics. I told him it wasn't going to be pretty and that he should really think about leaving. But Henry was determined to see his horse buried.

With the backhoe, I started smashing the horse into the ditch. It was really gross. A horrible smelling gas gushed out of the animal, and we could hear the bones breaking as the hydraulics went to work. The hard part was getting the head to smash down so that the animal was deep enough in the hole to put dirt over it. Henry tearfully hung in there until the horse was completely buried. I ran the backhoe back and forth on the loose dirt to pack it down. Henry then went home, and everybody went back to their trailers.

Henry's wife worked at the college and had told people about what had happened. After a couple of days the whole thing became a big joke. I started receiving pictures of horses in my mail slot in the faculty lounge. Employees at the college started dropping by my office and making jokes about the whole thing. It became the talk of the college. I started laughing about it myself. Henry even started joking about it. He said, "Bill, when I die, bury me out there with my ass sticking out of the ground to be used as a salt lick."

# - 35 -

# WHISKEY JACK AND THE DOGS

We called him "Whiskey Jack" because he was a full-blown alcoholic whose drink of choice was whiskey. He was kind of dirty and had long greasy grayish hair, a leathery face, and bloodshot eyes. Jack would never mess up the outdoor public toilet and shower because he never went in there to use the toilet and never took a shower. When Jack was sober, which was not too often, he was personable. He loved dogs and owned three, which he always kept in his small, rundown trailer. At about six in the morning he would let them out to do their business. Rarely did he put them on a leash.

One of his dogs was named "Little Bit" and was dreaded by the whole park. At six o'clock every morning Jack turned him loose, and the dog would mark almost every trailer in the park with a squirt on the tire. It was a mystery to me the capacity of this dog's bladder. He would ration himself and urinate on almost every trailer; the ones he missed he would get the next day. It was driving everyone crazy, and people were angry.

Jack claimed he had no control over the situation. Every morning at about six thirty, a half hour after the dog had been loose, Jack would yell at the top of his lungs, "Little Bit! Get your ass over here!" This would wake up a lot of people. Little Bit was a dog who would only respond to his master. He ignored everybody else who tried to run him off when he was urinating on their tires.

Jack was pretty much a loner and didn't really like other people. For a long time I suspected he would do things—nothing very serious—just to irritate the others. I suspect it gave him some sense of power. He was, however, respectful towards me, because I had threatened to kick him out on more than one occasion.

One afternoon I happened by his trailer. Jack's door was open, and he was inside with three very happy dogs. He stopped me and invited me in for a piece of cake, which he was slicing up in a filthy pan. He told me that every week he would bake the dogs a cake. When he asked if I wanted a piece, I politely said that I had just eaten and then went on my way. I don't think I had ever turned down a piece of cake before, but this time there was no way I was going to eat a piece of that dog cake.

One day I walked past Jack's trailer and saw a huge pit bull on a short rope lying outside. This dog was really scarred and was obviously a retired fighting dog. I said, "Jack, what is this dog doing here?" He said that he needed a home. He went on to warn me that this dog would kill anything that came near him and that he was one mean son of a bitch. I was admittedly a little shocked. So I said, "Jack, that is why you can't have this dog living here, and that is why he needs to leave now!" Jack answered that he had nowhere to take him and that he needed a home. I told Jack that the dog needed to leave or I was going to call the police. It was then that Jack said, "Okay, let me make a telephone call at the pay phone, and I will be right back."

I waited at his trailer to make sure nobody came close to this dog. When he returned, he told me he would take the dog to a dog lady who rescued pets but that he had no way to transport him. I told Jack we could tie him up in the back of my truck and take him there. We drove about fifteen miles, and he directed me to the dog lady's location. She lived in a double-wide trailer on about a half acre with a fenced-in yard. This place was way out in the country, kind of isolated from other neighbors.

When we got there I couldn't believe my eyes. I estimated that there were in excess of a hundred and fifty dogs in her half-acre yard. There were dogs fighting, dogs playing, dogs sleeping, dogs pooping, dogs humping each other, and a deafening bedlam of constant barking. At least three dogs were visible, peering through each window from the inside. This dog lady obviously loved dogs and had rescued a multitude of them. I do not know how she could afford to feed them all.

When we beeped the horn, the lady came out. She was hard to distinguish other than the fact that she was very big and had two legs. She seemed to be in her fifties with a long mane that covered most of her face. She kind of kicked her way through the crowd of dogs, screaming at them by name to get the hell out of the way. She accepted the dog from Jack and said she had a special fenced-in area to keep him separated and safe from the other dogs.

On the way back I thought that maybe I should contact the Humane Society, but the dogs looked healthy, and I knew that at the dog pound they would probably meet with certain death. If the dogs were accepted in the neighborhood, then I shouldn't be the one to report anybody.

I warned Jack again that if he even breathed without my approval, he would be out of the park. As it turned out, a short time later I saw him drunk and parading around the park carrying a huge, eighteen-inch knife strapped to his leg. When I confronted him he told me that in America he had the right to carry a weapon for his own safety. I told him that he was scaring the other residents and that I was revoking his rights and kicking him out of the park. And, yes, I told him that he would receive a hundred-dollar bill at the entrance when he drove out.

His eyes lit up. I guess thinking about how much whiskey he could purchase excited him.

# - 36 -

# THE THREE-MAN SLINGSHOT

During the initial planning and construction phase of the RV park, one of our neighbors on a ten-acre parcel close to the back was dead set against us building the park. They were sure it would ruin their property value, be ugly, pollute their well, be too noisy, and in general ruin their lifestyle.

The county set a date to hear each of our arguments and to make a decision about the building of the park. At the meeting all the arguments were presented and the county voted to continue the project regardless of our neighbor's objections. I think their decision was based more on the RV park generating revenue than on the concerns of the neighbors. As it turned out, none of their complaints were valid except possibly that the park ruined their view in one direction.

Afterward they continued to be quite hateful toward me and thought they should personally come onto our property on a regular basis to inspect the work being done. Each time it would generate a verbal altercation between us. When the park was in full operation we had a few residents including a few teenagers and my son living there. I had a very good relationship with these boys, and they rarely caused me grief. Oh, there were a few mischievous things that they did, but they would always adhere to my request to clean up whatever mess they would make. They were just good kids having fun.

It was no secret in the park that my neighbors had gone all out to stop construction and that they were being hateful toward me. So my son and two other boys decided to attack the neighbor's home with green oranges late one night. One of them had a three-man slingshot. One of the boys would hold a rubber strap on one side, another would hold the other rubber strap on the other side, and the third boy would pull back a connecting pouch that would fire about a dozen green oranges at a time. The range of this slingshot was a little more than a hundred yards.

One night between eleven and midnight the boys snuck out and set up their operation in the orange grove beside the house. They began loading and firing at a trajectory that would send green oranges raining down on top of the house. They bombarded our neighbor for about ten minutes. It was a very dark night, and the boys adjusted their trajectory based on listening to where the oranges were coming down. I found out later that the family who lived in house was scared to death while this was happening. It appeared to them that their home was totally surrounded by angry park people attacking them. To them it must have seemed similar to being surrounded by attacking Indians in an old western movie.

They called the police and reported the incident. The next day I explained the whole situation to the police, who decided that since nobody was hurt and there was no damage to the house, it was a minor crime. I promised the police that I would march the kids over there, have them apologize, and, if need be, do a little work picking up the oranges around the neighbor's house.

I am glad the orange grower next door had a sense of humor about the incident even though he was not happy with the loss of about a hundred oranges. I told him that I would pay him for his loss, but he declined my offer.

Obviously, I was upset at my son and his teenage friends who had waged this artillery barrage on the neighbors. At the same time, although I didn't tell them, I was touched by what they did. They did it for me because they cared about me. They were angry at the neighbors, and it was their way of fighting back at them for giving me a hard time. I had a long talk with them and convinced them that their actions were wrong and that they were fortunate that nobody was hurt and no damage was done. They promised me that they would never bother the neighbors again.

I did not confiscate the slingshot because, honestly, it was the coolest slingshot I had ever seen. It had four strands of large, special rubber bands on each side of a pouch about the size of a hollowed-out soccer ball. It had a handle on it for one person to pull it back and a handle on either side of the bands for two other people to hold. It was about five feet across, and, as I remember, it would stretch back about three feet. Why couldn't I have thought of building something like this when I was a kid?

They had a lot of fun after that, lobbing dirt clods and other objects out into the vacant field. I found out later they also had fired off a few frogs.

When I talked to the parents of these kids about the prank, they didn't seem to take the whole thing very seriously, and we all kind of laughed about it. It was probably nothing compared to the other trouble these kids had gotten into. I couldn't help but be concerned about what the future held for these kids given the fact that their parents were not the best role models in the world and that they lived in such poverty and ignorance. As I have mentioned, when you're living in poverty, there are usually many social problems that come included in the package.

# - 37 -

# ELECTRICAL PROBLEMS AND OTHER DANGERS

As poor people, the residents repaired their own dilapidated trailers and usually did an adequate job. Doing electrical repairs was often a disaster, though. They didn't know how electricity worked (watts, amps, resistance, wiring, grounding, etcetera). Typically a circuit or two would burn out, and the residents would buy multiple plug adapters and run extension cords to wherever they needed them. We were lucky that there were no trailer fires.

I wanted all electrical repairs to be done by an electrician, but still the residents would do their own and not let me know about it until there was a problem.

Bill and Martha lived off of her Social Security disability, and he worked seasonal jobs for cash under the table. I guess they had a faulty plug attached to the end of the umbilical cord that plugged into the electrical thirty-amp pedestal in between the trailer spaces. They bought a three-pronged plug to replace the old one, but when Bill did the repair he wired it wrong. That is, he wired the hot wire directly to the ground.

Word got to me that people were being seriously shocked getting in and out of that trailer; the second they had one foot on the ground and one foot on the trailer step, they would receive a shock, so they were afraid to enter or leave. Their dog didn't have a problem though, because he would jump from the ground into the trailer. Noticing this, they learned to take a little hop to the first step in order to avoid getting shocked.

I was worried that somebody was going to get electrocuted, but at first I didn't know what the problem was. All I knew was that the metal pedestal where Bill and Martha's cord was plugged in was very hot to the touch. Even the dirt around the pedestal was warm to the touch. I knew there was a major problem, and I knew that electricity was pouring into the ground, so I hired an electrician to come in to look at the problem.

When he touched his electric meter to the trailer, he discovered that the entire trailer was lit up with 110 volts. He then discovered that the plug on Bill's cord had been wired incorrectly, and he fixed the problem.

I don't think Bill and Martha understood the seriousness of the situation. They actually thought the whole thing was funny. In fact, I understood they would invite friends over without telling them about the problem. When they came in the trailer door, they would get a shock, and everybody would laugh.

# - 38 -

# GUNS IN THE PARK

Another potentially dangerous problem, especially with those who took drugs or frequently got drunk, was that the residents were armed. Most of the trailers had a loaded gun. This was a big secret that nobody wanted me to know about. In hindsight, I really don't know what I could have done about it anyway. The trailer walls were so thin that with an accidental discharge a bullet could probably have traveled through at least half a dozen trailers and hit me right in the ass. The fact that people were armed was probably my biggest denial, as I just tried not to think about it. Of course, I also had a gun in my motor home.

Another dangerous situation occurred shortly after a very nice, respectable couple in their sixties moved in. They had a nice trailer, so I put them in the front half of the park. About a week later they had two guests, a man and a woman in their forties, who they had picked up and brought to their trailer. I was fooled by these people because, as it turned out, they were big partiers.

One night at about one o'clock in the morning, there was quite a ruckus: yelling, screaming and doors slamming cut through the night air. I could hear it even though I was in my RV and in bed.

I immediately got dressed and walked out to see what the problem was, when I saw the guests walking out of the park entrance. The woman was trying to walk ahead of the staggering man, as if trying to get away. He would catch up to her, grab her, and try to strike her, but she would duck and pull away from him and keep walking. He went after her a couple of times, trying to physically abuse her. If I had taken the time to call the police I'm sure he would have succeeded in physically injuring this woman or perhaps even killing her, because he was in such a drunken rage.

I had my cell phone with me, so I jumped in my Jeep and drove after them. By this time, she was about twenty feet ahead of him. I drove up next to her and asked if she needed help. She could not get in the jeep fast enough. At that same time, the man ran to the driver's side and looked at me. While I was thinking about what the hell I was going to do if he opened the door, he then threw up his arms and said, "Take the bitch." I put it in gear and took off.

She burst into tears and told me that I was very lucky, because he had just gotten out of prison and was carrying a gun. I gasped a great sigh of relief as I sped away. I quickly called the police to report the incident, and I also called my wife to tell her to turn off the lights and lock the door. Our motor home was located right at the entrance, and I didn't want the man coming back.

The woman and I met the sheriff at a nearby gas station and told him what had happened. He assured us that he would search the park for him. I ended up driving the woman to her sister's house a few miles away and returned to the park as quickly as I could. The deputy called and told us that he could not find the armed man and that perhaps he had gone into the orange grove and passed out, but he would keep checking throughout the night.

My adrenaline was really pumping, thinking that I had come pretty close to being shot, and I was also worried that the man would return to the park. So I stayed awake, looking through the window, keeping watch on the entry. The man indeed returned, staggering through the entrance, probably to return to the trailer and the people he had been drinking with.

I told my wife to call the sheriff and tell him the man had returned. In the meantime, I decided to take my cell phone and follow him to see what he was up to and where he was going. He walked all over the place looking for this trailer, but he was so drunk he could not find it. I was worried about what he was going to do, but I knew the deputy would be there in just a couple of minutes to arrest him.

The man noticed I was following him, and he started toward me. My instincts told me that he probably would not recognize me, so I decided to have a friendly conversation with him to buy some time.

I remember watching a very funny movie with Gene Wilder called *Young Frankenstein*. There was a scene in the movie where Gene Wilder tries to befriend his creation by having his assistants lock the two of them in the same cell, making them promise that no matter what he said they should not open the cell door.

Remembering from the movie that Dr. Frankenstein, in his effort to survive, sweet-talked the monster, I utilized my counseling skills, and in a very friendly way said things like, "Hi. How are you tonight? You look like a very nice man who has had a run of bad luck. Is there any way I can help you tonight?"

He sat down on the lawn and began to tell me about his life. He said that out of his whole adult life there had only been two years that he was not incarcerated. He got quite emotional as he was telling me this. He then asked me to please drive him to the town eight miles away to his brother's house. I told him that I would but my wife was playing poker with some friends and had the car, but that she should be back any minute. He replied, "It's awfully late for her to be out playing poker."

I said that we had had a fight and that was the reason she had not returned home yet, but I knew she would be here any minute now. I talked to this man for about forty-five minutes, and still there was no deputy. The man started to get suspicious that I was stalling for time, and he confronted me about it.

Just then the deputy's car came flying through the driveway, and I flagged him down. He jumped out of the car with his gun drawn, yelling at the man to put his arms above his head and to remain lying down. The deputy rolled him over, put his arms behind his back, and put the handcuffs on. He searched him carefully but could not find the weapon. He put him in the car and apologized for not being able to come sooner; he was in the middle of an emergency. I thanked him, went back to my motor home and my worried wife, and went to bed.

The next morning, I had a couple of people help me look through the grove next to the road for the gun, but we could not find it. I was beginning not to enjoy this job.

# - 39 -

# BEING SHOT AT FROM THE HIGHWAY

When construction began on the RV park, we were living in a little house in the middle of the property about three hundred feet from the highway. It was about eleven at night, my daughter had a couple of girls over to spend the night, and they had just gone to bed. My wife was sitting up in bed reading, and I was in the living room watching the news. The blinds in the house were all shut, and the only light left on was the porch light. Usually I never left any lights on.

All of a sudden I heard a loud pop. Having been a combat soldier, I instantly knew what the noise was. It was the typical sound made when a bullet comes in your direction. The pop was actually the bullet breaking the sound barrier. I knew that someone had shot at the house.

I checked on the kids, and they were all right. I then went to our bedroom, where Joanne asked what the noise was. I told her that someone had shot at the house and that I was going to look around to see where the bullet had hit. I looked at the bedroom window first and found that the bullet had gone through it. I looked around in the bedroom and saw a bullet hole in the wall about a foot away from Joanne's chest. The trajectory of the bullet from the window to the wall had come across my wife's chest. The bullet went into the wall at an angle, coming close to hitting her.

I asked if she was okay and she said, "Yes," in a surprisingly calm manner. I suggested we both go to the living room and turn off the lights. I called the police, who showed up at our door in about fifteen minutes. A police officer took the report and said she would look around but did not expect to find anything. The gunshot had come from the highway that ran past our property. I think whoever fired the gun saw the porch light on and just fired at it.

The police officer returned and suggested that someone had shot from their automobile and that it was probably a random drive-by shooting. She was very surprised that my wife was calm about the whole thing. She said to call her if there were any more problems, and she would be right over. When she left, my wife began to tremble and cry. There was about an hour delayed reaction with her before the shock and fear kicked in.

We talked for a while, had a glass of wine, and she went to bed. She was okay. I, on the other hand, stayed up all night sitting on the couch and listening with a gun beside me.

The girls and my son had slept through the whole thing.

I felt extremely angry. Here I was home from a combat zone, and someone had fired a shot into my house. My family had been violated, and my wife had almost been killed. I regretted that I did not have the chance to return the fire. It bothered me that I was living in an unsafe area, and I thought about it all night long. I went over many ideas in my head on ways to make this small town and the outlying areas safer.

I knew that the small community about two miles away was kind of lawless. There were a lot of people who would often fire weapons during the night. I don't think anybody was actually being shot, or at least I didn't see any evidence of that on the news. It appeared that people just liked to shoot their weapons once in a while. They knew it would take the police at least ten to fifteen minutes to arrive from the town, which was eight miles away. They knew they could get away with almost anything because of the absence of police in the area.

There was one account of someone walking down a street with houses on both sides, pulling a pistol from a holster, firing into a tree, and then just walking away. There were a sufficient number of incidents over a long period to cause the residents to become desensitized, making them not really motivated to call the police.

One day my junior high school daughter and I drove to the only restaurant in town, which had a drive-through window in the back. We had just placed our order when a school bus stopped to drop off high school students from the next town over. The kids who got off the bus (about twelve to fifteen of them) were all Hispanic males, unlike the mostly Caucasian kids who lived at the RV park.

As we waited for our food, it became apparent that these kids were part of a gang accompanying their leader, who they all related to in a respectful manner. The leader stood fairly close to our car. He took off his shirt, exposing a muscular body, while all the other boys formed a line to walk past him. Each kid paid his respects to the leader with a special handshake.

My daughter and I knew it was a local gang who had committed some crimes and violent acts in our little town. My daughter became really scared and said, "Dad, don't look at them. Let's just get out of here." Just looking at them could be interpreted as a threat. But the gang really didn't act like they were threatened by us. Actually it seemed as if they were putting on a little performance for us.

While my daughter understood how serious it was to stare at these people, I had a hard time keeping my eyes off of them. I had never witnessed firsthand, and up close, a social ritual of a gang. These kids were absolutely enthralled and seemed to worship this leader. The gang members obviously felt good about their involvement. I think they gained a sense of identity. Belonging to the gang and conforming to the leader's expectations gave them all a sense of meaning and worth that they didn't receive at home. I understood that the followers would probably do anything this authority figure asked them to do.

After this ritual the boys just kind of dispersed. As my son-in-law says, "The loyalty and obedience of the gang is excellent, but the leadership is very bad." Kids in gangs all over the country need better mentors.

This brings me back to one of my theories: If the government decreased NASA's budget by one half, put all that money into hiring social workers and students of social work, and placed them in towns and cities all over the country specifically to organize the youth and involve them in positive activities, it would make a difference.

I made an appointment to speak with the school's principal. My kids were both students at that school, and my wife had a full-time teaching position there in special education and second grade. I had known the principal and had heard about him from many years back when he was a student at the college where I worked. He had become an elementary school teacher and, in fact, my daughter had been one of his students. Now he was principal of the middle school.

Mr. Bentley was extremely effective with students and staff, knew many people in the community, and was very concerned about student welfare. He believed the educational institution needed to be central to the community. He wanted to make the school district an integral part of the community and the community an integral part of the schools in order to stop the growing gang problem. The success of the school district depended on working with the community and being a part of it in the most positive and productive way possible.

I talked to him, and he agreed that both of us working together could develop a town council. This council would be official and operate like a regular city council, working closely with the police. It would oversee the affairs of the community, organize programs, develop policies to facilitate the operation of these programs, and improve the general safety of the town's residents. This was not going to be an easy undertaking because most of the town's population consisted of migrant families who did seasonal work in agriculture. Many were illegal immigrants who worked hard to support their families but needed to stay under the radar of the authorities.

Our town was suffering from a phenomenon sociologists call "Concentric Zone Theory": The original people in the town had slowly moved out into the surrounding rural areas, leaving a void in the town to be filled by people who were on a much lower socioeconomic level. One can see this theory in progress by looking at what happened to downtown LA or any other major city that has become an inner-city slum. What had happened to this town was the same thing, except on a much smaller scale.

The principal and I met with several individuals who we saw as leaders in the community. We created flyers announcing a meeting concerning the development and formation of the new council and put them up all over town. The first meeting, held in the school cafeteria, drew approximately fifty people. The idea went over big, so a time and place for the election of a town council was scheduled. We did not use ballots for this election. The people who were nominated as board members stood in the front with their backs to the voting body so they could not see people actually voting by show of hands.

We had recruited the county sheriff and a friend of mine who had retired from the college to count the votes. That night five town council board members were elected. One of the elected board members was overwhelmed with feelings of patriotism and with tears in his eyes said, "Only in America could this raw democratic process take place." The news of our budding town council made the main newspaper in the county. Our small town got behind the council, and it really took off.

One of its accomplishments was convincing the county supervisors that the assignment of a law enforcement officer who actually lived in the town would make a world of difference to the peace of the community. The county agreed to transfer one of its deputies for this purpose.

This deputy was just the right person. He spoke Spanish and related well to the kids, residents, and school alike. He was involved in the community and attended town council meetings. This man made a big difference right away. Crime dropped, and very little gunfire could be heard after that. A park built by volunteers was a place where people could go to play soccer and volleyball, have barbecues, and more. Of course the school worked closely with the council, and the problems of this little town were greatly diminished after that.

# - 40 -

## COCKROACH GARY

We first met Gary when he walked into the RV park. He had been beaten up and said that he had paid somebody to move his trailer to the area, but the man had disconnected him about a mile away, took his money, and left.

We guessed that he was mentally ill by his odd demeanor. He was agitated and trembling and had difficulty communicating. Chubby and short in stature, he also had difficulty walking. As he moved about he gave the appearance of someone who had tripped on something and was leaning forward in an attempt to catch his balance. By his unkempt appearance and lack of hygiene, he was obviously someone who was having a hard time taking care of himself.

He told us that he had a steady income on Social Security disability, and he needed a safe place to set up his trailer and to live. He said he had no other place to go at that time, and he was half begging and half promising that he would be no problem if we would allow him to live in our park.

My wife and I assessed that he would not be a danger to anyone. I told him that I would drive with him over to see his trailer, and we would figure out, based on what his trailer looked like, whether he could stay or not. I looked at the trailer, which proved to be barely passable, and agreed to let him stay. We had a space a bit out of the way in the back where he could live and where people would not really notice. We just didn't have the heart to turn him away, and so we decided to give it a try.

When Gary went to town about eight miles away to shop, he would usually hitch a ride with someone—even though nobody wanted him in their vehicle because of his lack of hygiene. However, people generally had compassion for Gary and would give him a ride.

After his business was taken care of in town, he would try to hitch a ride back on the highway going out of the town. If he had trouble getting picked up, he would fake a medical problem. From time to time residents from the RV park would observe him walking out into the road and stopping traffic by staggering around, holding his stomach as if he were in pain, or faking a heart attack by clutching his hands to his chest. Concerned citizens would often stop to help him. Apparently, if someone wanted to call an ambulance, he would insist that he would be better in a while and did not want to go to the hospital. This was a pretty clever scheme, and he always succeeded in getting home.

I had talked to Gary several times about practicing better hygiene, but he never did get the message. He started bringing home stray cats, sneaking them into his trailer. He loved those cats, and if you stood outside his trailer, you could hear him talking to them as if they were children. I told him that eight cats living in his trailer was a little much, but I figured that since he never let them outside, nobody would know the difference. He did promise me that he would not bring any more cats home, and he understood that he would have to leave if he did.

In time, his trailer started to smell pretty bad, and his neighbors started to complain. After making him clean the inside of his trailer, the situation would be okay for a while, but in a couple of weeks the smell would start permeating from his trailer again.

He started attracting cockroaches, which, as most people know, multiply prolifically. Gary didn't mind the cockroaches. A few times people would point out to him that he had cockroaches climbing all over him. He would say, "Well, they need a place to live, too."

It was not long before I gave him notice that he would have to leave. While people cared about him, they could no longer tolerate his filth. I was concerned that he was contaminating the whole park with roaches. People did not want to use the shower after him, even though he only took a shower about once or twice a month. People did not want him using the washing machine and dryer, thinking that he would contaminate their clothes. Gary's hygiene and cat problems finally outweighed my compassion and concern for him.

He reported to me that he intended to sell his trailer and move into a low-rent motel in Porterville that housed the unfortunate and the street people as long as they could pay a small rental fee. My first thought was to wonder who in the world would be crazy enough to buy his cockroach-filled trailer. Believe it or not, somebody did buy it in just a few days and hauled it off. I did not think it was even worth ten dollars.

Everybody was so happy to see Gary and the trailer leave that we threw a potluck. I bought a case of cockroach killer and enlisted about five volunteers to spray his space and the surrounding area as the trailer was pulling out, while other volunteers followed it along as it drove away, killing any cockroaches that fell from it onto the park road. As the trailer pulled out, the ground under it became alive with thousands of cockroaches. People with the spray cans, including myself, were freaked out as we frantically sprayed the ground moving under our feet. We did this three separate times until we could no longer see anything moving.

We never saw Gary again after that. During most of his stay with us, the higher class people in the front were not aware of his problems. Had they known, I think it would have hurt our business badly. I was growing weary and definitely did not like this RV park job any longer.

# - 41 -

# BILL'S PERCEIVED ARREST

On my way to town one time, I stopped at the corner to fill up my diesel truck. I had travelled only a mile toward town when the engine started sputtering and making noise. Pulling over, I turned off the engine, thinking there might be serious damage occurring. I lifted the hood and inspected the engine, which seemed to be all right. It was not overheating, and there was no oil leaking.

I stood there scratching my head, surprised, because this truck was in very good condition. I thought for a few minutes before the light bulb came on in my head. Had I mistakenly filled my tank with gasoline instead of diesel fuel? I took the fuel cap off and smelled. I had indeed filled the tank with gasoline. A diesel engine will not run on gas. I could not believe I had done something so incredibly stupid.

A highway patrolman pulled over and asked me if I was having a problem. I told him what I had accidentally done. He kindly helped me call a tow truck to haul it to my mechanic. Being the helpful man he was, he offered to give me a ride back to the park, which I greatly appreciated.

When we pulled into the park I gave him a quick tour of the place, proudly displaying the landscaping and the tidiness of the place. He drove me to my motor home to drop me off. We talked for a few minutes, because I knew his father-in-law, who owned a crop spraying business a few miles away. As we were chatting I noticed that a few people were beginning to gather, and I noticed others were looking at us from their trailers. I thanked the officer for his help and went into my motor home.

Word spread in the park like fire that I had been arrested. From their experiences, if you were riding in a police car, you surely had to have been arrested.

Their reaction struck me and my wife funny, and even after I explained what happened, many of the residents refused to believe that I was not in some kind of trouble with the police. I guess our realities are based primarily on our experiences.

# - 42 -

# THE MUSHROOM PEOPLE

Every spring the mushroom people from Oregon would show up and stay for a month or two. They made a living by traveling from place to place picking wild mushrooms. Every other day they would drive to the Fresno airport and fly the mushrooms to special warehouses where they would be bought and distributed all over the country. I was told that exclusive restaurants would purchase these rare mushrooms and pay as much as sixty dollars per pound for them. Until these mushroom people showed up, I had no idea that there was a wild mushroom industry.

Certain types of wild mushrooms grow in different geographical areas at different times of the year. The particular mushrooms they were looking for in our area were called morels. As they explained it, they grow mostly in olive orchards and only under the right conditions. For the mushrooms to manifest, the olive trees have to be pruned a year or more beforehand with the slash material left on the ground to decompose. The olive orchards that were picked up after pruning grew no mushrooms.

This band of people knew exactly which groves produced these mushrooms. They would get permission from the growers to go into their groves to harvest them. It was absolutely secret where the groves were located. There were probably fifteen out of maybe a hundred groves where the mushrooms grew and where arrangements had been made with the growers to pick on their property. Again, the locations of these special olive groves were top secret.

In the early morning when the mushroom pickers would head out to a location, they would watch in their rearview mirrors to see if they were being followed by rival pickers. If they were to detect a rival they would purposely take wrong turns and try to confuse their pursuers.

There were many other groups of pickers that operated in this fashion independent of the Oregon people, but they all indirectly actually worked together. Some of the pickers would sneak into the olive groves to look for mushrooms without the approval of the landowner.

Only the mushroom people from Oregon had the connections and knew which warehouse to fly the mushrooms to. All the other pickers would sell their mushrooms to the Oregon people, who would buy them for around six dollars a pound.

Here is how the whole thing worked. The mushroom people would show up at the park, rent a space or two, and set up a twelve-by-twelve-foot tent equipped with a couple of tables and a calibrated scale. They also had special containers in which to ship the mushrooms. All the pickers, including the people from Oregon, would leave early in the morning and pick until dark. That evening the local pickers would converge on the tent to sell their mushrooms. Some of the pickers had harvested enough to be worth a few hundred

BILL ROBERTS

dollars. Others had not found any that day. Still others had found only a few pounds. After the mushroom business was completed in the tent, they would all celebrate by lifting a few beers.

Morel mushrooms look like little bumps on the ground that are about a couple inches wide and a couple inches tall. They are dark and hard to see, but all have the same characteristic little point on the top. To find them the pickers would have to stoop down very low to the ground, looking for areas with clumps of little pointed tops sticking out of the ground.

All of the pickers seemed to know each other since they did this every year. There were a variety of people with different lifestyles who participated in this yearly mushroom ritual. While they appeared to be friendly with each other, there was an underlying distrust and subtle competitiveness among them. The Oregon people who facilitated all this had to guard their mushrooms carefully until they were loaded in a couple of vans to be taken to the airport for shipping.

Near the end of the season, which, again, only lasted a month or two, the harvesting would slow down and everybody would start having a lot of fun. The mushroom pickers from Oregon were really a bunch of fine people. There were five of them who lived in two trailers. There was a married couple who lived in one trailer, a woman who appeared to be the boss who lived in the other trailer with her elderly mother, and a young lady in her twenties who seemed to be a friend of the family. We sat around in the evening and socialized, drinking beer and eating a few mushrooms cooked in various ways. They tasted very good, but I didn't understand why exclusive restaurants were willing to pay sixty dollars a pound for them.

The mushroom people could be described as honest and very down-to-earth. They had hearty laughs and often played practical jokes on each other—and on me. They got me good a couple of times, and I them.

They had a chihuahua named Jose that was an ankle-biting, hateful, little dog. I could not get near him without him acting like he wanted to kill me. Most people were afraid of this little dog, especially me. While the dog tolerated most people, he absolutely hated me.

After the season, the mushroom people would return to their homes and families in Oregon. I don't know how many months per year they traveled around picking various wild mushrooms, but their income was obviously substantial enough to sustain them or they would not be in the business. In the five years that we operated the park, we looked forward to seeing them each season.

# - 43 -

# CLANS

The people of the RV park who were poor, which was probably two-thirds of the residents, knew how to survive. I believe there were basically three clans who lived there. There was the Jake and Marie clan, the Pearl and Bert clan, and the carnie clan. I am defining a clan as many relatives living in close proximity to one another. They lived in the rear section of the park, each of the families having their own trailer.

The rent at the park was low, and it was an ideal way for poor people to live. Family members were also right there to assist each other, helping with child care, helping somebody who might be ill, sharing food when necessary, sharing values, social events, family traditions, transportation, and more. Living in close proximity rather than scattered apart afforded them an easier and more comfortable means of survival.

These three clans mingled and socialized together. It may be that the three clans had a couple of distant relatives in the past who connected most of them. I heard some talk about that, but I am not sure if this was truly the case. If so, then they were actually one big family. Their lifestyle was fascinating to me and sparked my interest.

These were all good people, and my wife and I grew to like them. They bought their clothes from secondhand stores, they loved their kids and each other like anybody else would, and they knew how to have simple fun. They were not in any way cliquish; outsiders were always welcome. There didn't seem to be any effort to achieve social status because they had no social status.

They did not seem to be in competition with each other about ordinary things such as who had the nicest trailer or automobile, nor were they trying to "keep up with the Joneses." They lived from week to week, maybe day to day, with no apparent plans for the future. They seemed to know who they were and seemed to be proud of their cultural ways.

They did not steal from each other, and they all seemed to get along harmoniously, for the most part. Rarely were there any problems among them, but when there was a problem, it was usually pretty serious.

# - 44 -

# THE BIG FIGHT

One weekend Marie and Jake had invited a young lady who was a cousin of theirs to spend the night. She was probably twenty years old and lived about thirty miles away.

I was awakened at about midnight one time by screaming and fighting by the restroom and shower area. Marie and her cousin were drunk and involved in a terrible physical and verbal altercation; they were pulling each other's hair out and punching each other repeatedly in the face, with vulgarities flying.

There was no time for me to call the police, and I felt I had to stop this fight before any serious injuries occurred. I was giving them verbal commands and trying to get right between them to break it up, with little success. If I restrained one of them the other would come after her. There was nobody to help me because it was late and everybody was in bed.

Pretty soon they were both exhausted, and the fight stopped temporarily. I was relieved when they stopped, because I had also been roughed up and hit a few times. This young girl had been dropped off at the park by relatives and was stuck without a ride home.

The only way I could prevent them from continuing their feud was to separate them by taking the young girl to our motor home. She called her mother, crying, trying to explain what had happened. Her mother said that she and a couple of friends were on their way to pick her up. She also let it be known that they were going to beat the daylights out of Marie to settle the matter.

When there was a problem in the park, I rarely called the police, because I didn't want the business to get a bad reputation in the county. I decided to try to prevent any further conflict and to make sure this girl was taken home.

In about an hour, a four-door sixties-model Oldsmobile pulled in through the gate and stopped at the entrance, not knowing which trailer to go to. I came out of our motor home with the girl to make sure she got in the car and to see that they were all on their way home.

The three women who showed up in the Oldsmobile were big mamas; they looked hefty and strong. They were mad as hell and had come to fight. I told them I was very sorry about what had happened and that I would get to the bottom of it in the morning. One especially mean-looking woman put her arm through the window and pointed her finger in my face and said, "We're going to get her, and you better not try to stop us."

I was fearful that these three women were going to get out of the car and physically assault me. I had never been in a fist-fight with three big women before. This would be a new experience but one that I certainly was not looking forward to. I thought I had better come up with something fast or run to the motor home and call the police. Knowing it would take a dreadfully long time for them to arrive, I told the women, "Look, I know you're very nice ladies, and the last thing I want to do is to have to call the police."

I said they had no reason to fight because the young girl had really gotten the best of Marie and that she had kicked her butt all over the RV park. I told them Marie was in her trailer licking her wounds, unable to fight anymore. The young drunken girl lit up with pride when I said that, and the others felt some measure of satisfaction at that point. After thinking about it for a minute or two longer they decided to take the young girl and leave. I breathed a sigh of relief and went back to the safety of the motor home.

Truthfully, I believed Marie had gotten the best of the young girl, but I had averted more problems, so I went to bed planning on speaking to Marie in the morning.

The next day Marie apologized and said that they had both drunk too much that night and that she would never do that again. This was the first time in the two years Marie had lived in the park that she had ever caused a problem. Because of this, and because she was so sincerely apologetic, I forgave her.

For most of the next day the citizens of the park were involved in post-fight conversations. In the midst of all the gossip I learned that there had been a long history of problems between the two families, but, true to her word, Marie never caused another scene like that again.

# - 45 -

# MARIE'S DEATH

As I mentioned before, every night Marie would take a plate of food to San Quentin Larry in the back corner of the park. He would often visit Marie and her husband, Jake, at their trailer, because they were longtime friends. Larry lived a clean and sober life after having been involved in a drug rehabilitation program at the county methadone clinic. Much to our surprise, six months after Marie's marriage to Jake, she moved in with Larry. I guess Jake's alcoholism got to be too much for her, and I think over time she had fallen in love with Larry.

During the six months she lived with Jake after their wedding, Marie's health suddenly deteriorated, and she became wheelchair-bound. Perhaps part of Marie's motivation to move in with Larry was that he was willing to take care of her, which Jake was probably incapable of doing. Sadly, about a month after Marie moved in with Larry she died suddenly.

She was one of many in the park who had lived their lives caught in a prison of ignorance and without medical care except for occasional trips to the emergency room. She was a smart and extremely sweet person, except when she drank. She had had a hard background of many years of drug abuse.

Growing up poor, she did not have nearly the amount of chances to succeed that the middle class enjoyed. One can make the argument that in America, you can succeed even if you are poor. That may be true for some, but from first-hand observation, I believe that, overall, the probability of poor people succeeding is much lower than for the middle class. Statistics will bear me out.

The people in the park were shocked and devastated, because they all loved Marie. Her husband, Jake, became extremely angry after her death, and soon after he walked over to Larry's trailer and got into a pretty serious altercation.

Joanne and I were gone at that time, but after that Larry immediately moved out.

We were not there for the funeral. I think Dr. Rice, who had married Jake and Marie, performed the ceremony.

# - 46 -

# INSECTS AND OTHER
# LIVING THINGS

Being located in an agricultural area seemed to bring on unique problems each year. After one extremely wet year, the park had a sudden, almost biblical-proportion infestation of frogs. These frogs just showed up one day. They were as big as three to four inches and numbered in the thousands, so we had to walk very carefully on the roads in order to avoid stepping on them. Hundreds of road-kill frogs covered the park. Every couple of days I would shovel them up and bury them in the field next to us. The health department told me this was a natural occurrence after a very wet winter and not to worry about it.

Another year we had a similar infestation of crickets. I hired a couple of people to spray in areas like the bathroom and laundry room. We would then sweep them into piles, throw a little gasoline on them, and burn them. There were so many crickets that they put off a very unpleasant odor. We had to be very selective about where we sprayed because I did not want to expose the kids to the poison. Luckily that infestation did not last for more than a few weeks, which was a great relief.

# - 47 -

# THE FLY EPIDEMIC

L iving in an agricultural area definitely had its disadvantages. There was a pistachio plant a couple of miles away that employed some of the park's residents for a few months during the season. This plant owned about twenty acres of open land about a half mile or so from the park. Pistachios have husks that are usually spread on the field and plowed under for fertilization.

One year after spreading the husks on the ground, they neglected to plow them under, which caused a horrible odor that spread for miles. After several days of this rotten stench, the flies began to multiply. After about a week, the flies numbered in the billions. They actually impaired the vision of people driving by the field; it was like driving in thick fog. They rapidly spread through the groves and into our park.

Joanne and I were out of town at the time and did not know about any of this. The woman who was watching the place as temporary manager never let us know—even when we talked on the phone to see how things were going in the park.

When we got back we were shocked at how the whole park had been taken over by these flies. The outer walls of the trailers were so thick with them that it looked as though they had been painted a dirty dark color. Hundreds of flies swarmed into cars and trailers as people attempted to get in or out of them. We felt sickened by the sight and felt as if we were in the middle of a nightmarish science fiction movie.

I immediately called the health department, who told me they had received calls from the whole town and that there was nothing they could do about it, although they did fine the pistachio company heavily for what had happened.

They told me to do the best I could—whatever that was—and that the problem would clear up in a couple of weeks. The health department did require the pistachio company to plow under the rotten husks, but by that time the harm had already been done.

# - 48 -

## GAY RICK

Rick was the only openly gay man in the park. While he was not flamboyantly gay, he did not mind letting everybody know in his conversations with people in the park. He was such a nice guy, nobody seemed to care.

He would come over to visit our motor home and get into long conversations with my wife at least a couple of times a week. A few people would talk to her on a regular basis. She was a great counselor. Joanne made them feel good and recognized them as the good people that they were.

Rick had grown up in the South in a nice home and was a regular at church. He had a good life until his homosexuality was found out. From that day forth, he was ostracized by his family, his church, and the rest of his community, so he moved out to California, where he never really settled into a career that he liked.

He lived with and was taken care of for a while by an older gay gentleman in the town about twenty miles away. The relationship did not work out, so he moved around with his trailer, finally ending up at our RV park. He did not cause any problems, and once in a while he would have a male friend over.

One morning his neighbor in the trailer next to him complained of hearing late night noises. I did not ask to have those noises described to me. The neighbor said that when she pulled her curtain back and looked next door into the window of Rick's trailer, she saw one man humping the other from behind. She said it made her sick, and she demanded to move to another space. She didn't admit it, but I think she had a little voyeuristic interest because she didn't follow up on moving to another space after all.

I talked to Rick about it the next day and asked him to be a little quieter and more discreet about his sexual activities. He understood that neighbors were awfully close to each other in an RV park setting, apologized, and admitted that he just got carried away.

As I mentioned, my wife, Joanne, talked with him often, and she expressed her concern that Rick was, to some degree, suicidal. We found out later that Rick was fighting for his life. He had contracted AIDS a few years before. He was fairly happy most of the time, but at times he got pretty low, scared, and depressed. In time, open sores became pronounced on his face, neck, hands, and arms. His fear and depression grew along with these open wounds. He tried to cover them without much success. He was becoming sicker, with no family or lover to turn to for help. He was alone and scared.

When Joanne and I were no longer living there, we heard that Rick had driven his car into the orange grove next to the park. According to witnesses, he took a bottle of propane with him in the car and apparently caused the tank to release the gas, with the windows rolled up. He then ignited the propane, which exploded, blowing him out through the windshield, causing serious burns and other injuries. He had to be flown out in a med-evac helicopter, and nobody heard from him again until a year later. He returned to the park healed of his burns and injuries and wanted to move back in. The new park management did not want him back.

# - 49 -

## PEARL AND BERT

Pearl and Bert had lived at the park for about two years. Sometimes their nineteen-year-old daughter and twenty-something son lived with them between jobs. There were plenty of others from their clan who would visit frequently. Pearl, who was in her forties, was a kind, loving person. She was jovial and funny and loved to cook for people who came over. Pearl had been married before to a man who was very violent and who physically abused her and the kids. She had told me this but never got into any of the details.

Her new husband, Bert, was a good man who was always helpful to those around him. He was also very funny and would entertain people with his sense of humor and personality. Bert worked at the nut processing plant on a seasonal basis. He also worked wherever he could doing odd jobs to pay the bills.

I didn't know it at the time, but Bert also sold drugs occasionally. He kept that hidden, and nobody ever said anything to me about it. I suspected a few times that he was under the influence of something, but I didn't know what it was. It could have been alcohol for all I knew. As long as he didn't cause a disturbance, it was none of my business.

Pearl and Bert had a great relationship and loved their family. They were never a problem in the park. There were a few people in the park who smoked marijuana. I could catch a whiff of it when I made my rounds in the evening, but I didn't know which trailer it was coming from. I would rather they smoked marijuana than get wild and crazy on alcohol. Besides, my job wasn't to catch people and have them arrested for breaking the law unless it was causing problems or becoming a safety issue for other residents in the park.

Pearl and Bert's daughter was the only one in the family who was making an effort to make something of herself. I know she attended community college on and off but had not found her niche. She ended up getting married and moving out of state. She would call me occasionally to let me know how things were going. I think she was trying to break out of the redneck culture and wanted something better in life.

I hope I am not stereotyping the Oaky culture (for lack of a better term), but, speaking in general, a lot of people from that culture did not appear to have a lot of drive to get ahead.

Their son, who I did not know very well, was quiet and had a serious nature. I always thought that he carried around a lot of anger, maybe from his background of abuse, but that is just my guess.

Well, tragedy hit the Pearl and Bert family. Bert got cancer and died about six months later. Not having any medical insurance, his treatment was undoubtedly substandard at best. That's just the way it is for poor people. When they get seriously ill in this country, the attitude is they can "eat shit and die."

I think for the most part there is a prevalent attitude among people who are doing well economically that poor people get themselves into this position, so they kind of have it coming to them. I have heard this throughout my life and more frequently as time has gone by. The belief is that those who work hard are rewarded with success by God's grace, and those who don't are not worthy of his grace because they are lazy and something must be wrong with them. This attitude stems from the Protestant work ethic, a concept in social science.

Around that same time, Pearl's son murdered his girlfriend in a rage. He then went up into the hills and killed himself. Pearl moved her trailer to another RV park. She lives alone, will not return phone calls, and will not answer the door. She was such a sweet person, and her situation sickens me.

# 50

# SELLING THE PARK

My brother and I and our wives were in Arizona, sitting outside our RV drinking beer, when I got a call. The caller introduced himself as an attorney. He said he had driven through our RV park, had talked to the people, and he wanted to buy it. I told him I hadn't really thought about selling it. He told me to think about it; he would call me back in the morning.

As we drank more beer, we talked about it. Joanne and I were getting tired of all the hard work; the heaviness of irresolvable problems people faced was getting us down. Also, our daughter had married and moved away. To be free to live closer to her was a thought that began to pull at our heartstrings. We were retired. We didn't need to work anymore, so we made the decision to sell the park and to drive away into the sunset.

The next morning we received the call from the attorney. We gave him our price, which he accepted immediately. We headed for home to close the deal. Being an attorney, he drew up the papers himself, which we took to a real estate attorney. After satisfying his bank's financial requirements as well as all the escrow requirements, the park had a new owner. We had cash in the bank and needed only to stay for two more weeks to teach the owner the operation.

On our final day, the residents gave us one last potluck, and the next morning we drove through the park blasting our horn and waving goodbye to everyone.

We were saddened to be moving away from the community we had developed. We had grown to love these people, but at the same time we were overwhelmed with excitement for the future.

# 51

# PRESIDENT JOHNSON, SECRETARY OF DEFENSE MCNAMARA, GENERAL WESTMORELAND, AND ME

When I read McNamara's book *In Retrospect*, I was beside myself with anger and disbelief, realizing that I had been on the receiving end of lies and deception. Unlike so many others who died in Vietnam, I escaped with my life, although by the skin of my teeth.

While there were many others involved in masterminding the war effort including the Cabinet, the Joint Chiefs of Staff, and other generals, it was President Lyndon B. Johnson, Secretary of Defense Robert McNamara, and General William Westmoreland who stand out as the main players responsible for the continuation of the war. Because of ego, politics, image, hubris, and a basic and total disregard for honesty and human life they hid the truth from Congress and the American people. They were also absolutely ignorant of Vietnamese culture.

Because of their ignorance and moral failings, hundreds of thousands of human beings died unnecessarily. I was convinced after reading this book that all three of these men knew from the beginning that we could not win that war.

I will offer my opinions, my brief take on the book, and do the best I can to paraphrase what I read as I understand it.

In 1965 President Johnson decided to escalate the war because the situation in South Vietnam, despite the intervention and support of the U.S. military, was deteriorating and heading toward defeat. Johnson did not want the world to think we were failing. He was worried about our international prestige being at risk.

He couldn't turn the war over to the South Vietnamese military, because their generals couldn't get along with each other, were incompetent, and not committed enough to win. He did not want to pull out, because it would have looked like surrender.

For years, upon McNamara's and Westmoreland's advice, LBJ had been building up troop levels and carrying on a massive bombing campaign while hiding this from Congress and the American public (McNamara 171).

For years he got the support of the American people for the war based on the domino theory that communist aggression would spread from country to country and eventually invade our shores if we didn't stop it there. For decades that evil word, communism, had caused Americans' hair to stand up on the backs of their necks. The memory of the McCarthy era of the fifties was still fresh in our minds, a time when we were told that a communist cancer was spreading into this country, and a witch-hunt had ensued.

For the next few years, LBJ continued to keep this whole thing a secret for political reasons. He was trying to get funding approved for his "Great Society" social agenda. This agenda encompassed immigration reform, the "War on Poverty," including aid to Appalachia and Medicare, and the Clean Air Act (McNamara 198).

He was also under pressure from hard-line conservatives and democrats alike to take far riskier action against North Vietnam. However, there was always the possibility of triggering a nuclear war with China or Russia, who were both supporting North Vietnam.

LBJ, upon Westmoreland's requests, continued to pour more and more troops and bombs into the war. Westmoreland "recommended the US take whatever measures . . . necessary to postpone indefinitely the day of collapse" (McNamara 177). Wow! He was saying we could not win the war, and yet he continued to advise Johnson to commit more troops and drop more bombs, intensifying and prolonging the war at tremendous human cost.

The buildup continued until there were more than a half million troops deployed, and we had actually dropped more bombs than during World War II. They knew they could not stop the North Vietnamese military and their supplies from entering South Vietnam. The American military could not break their spirit, and there could be no negotiation.

To say the whole thing was a disaster of epic proportion is a total understatement.

The individual who brought Johnson's presidency down, causing him not to run for reelection, was Daniel Ellsberg, a former captain and veteran of the war who had done three tours of duty and who later worked at the Pentagon. Ellsberg, as part of his job, had privileged access to White House information and communications. For moral reasons, and despite thinking he would surely go to prison, he courageously snuck out seven thousand top secret Pentagon papers, which showed what was really going on with the war as well as the lies and deception formulated by the president for Congress and the American public.

The papers clearly showed how much of the war the public didn't know about. President Nixon was temporarily successful later in legally stopping further publication of the papers through a ruling by a federal court, and Ellsberg was arrested. Later the Supreme Court ruled to continue the publications, citing the First Amendment.

According to a Public Broadcasting Service interview, Nixon wanted to get the "SOB" by breaking into Ellsberg's psychiatrist's office to find something to discredit him. This became known as the Watergate Scandal.

The public exposure of this truth, I believe, was the biggest reason for the beginning of the anti-war movement and a cultural revolution in this country. The news media published the papers and went after LBJ, McNamara, and Westmoreland. This started massive anti-war demonstrations at colleges, universities, in Washington, DC, and all over the country, causing heightened public awareness. President Johnson announced he would not run for re-election. McNamara announced he would retire, bringing his career to an end.

While he does admit mistakes, I believe McNamara's book was an effort to cover himself as best he could from his involvement and wrong decisions as Secretary of Defense during the war. Ellsburg named him "The President's Man."

In the end, I think McNamara mostly blamed Johnson for the mistakes.

Reading his writings, it was easy to get lost in his complexity and detail. The president, Westmoreland, and McNamara wrote myriads of memos to each other during the war. Johnson kept sending people who held prestigious positions to visit Vietnam to see how the war was going, and they would all report back the usual bad news that it wasn't going well. Then McNamara would write up a new plan and strategy with new goals and objectives, which he did over and over again.

The memos were written as if their contents were the gospel truth; they were written with great finesse and "wisdom" and sounded incredibly convincing. Men who are that important have to write great memos, you know.

Through it all, these men seemed incredibly removed from the toll of suffering and mass slaughter they were exacting. I got the impression that they were all playing a game of sorts, and, in some strange way, competing for control through these memos. The best sounding ideas and plans would win over the others. But ultimately the president had the last word. I wonder if these men ever cried or lost sleep or suffered remorse, thinking, "Oh my God, what have I done? How can I ever live with this?"

It would make sense to me that possibly these men were the extremes of sociopathic, narcissistic monsters, lost in their own worlds of self-importance, having little or no empathy or regard for the human suffering that was brought about by their own hands. This is my impression. I guess I will never know for sure what was going on in their heads. What I do

BEYOND MEDALS OF VALOR

know is that I lost dear friends needlessly in that war. I am still grieving and damned upset about it.

During the war those three men were putting unbelievable pressure on the troops to make progress at all costs, knowing the entire time their efforts would be consistently unsuccessful. That was why I and my fellow troops were in the field twenty-four hours a day, seven days a week, month after month.

McNamara wrote in his book that he got the idea to order an insane body count of the enemy to show with numbers how well we were doing. We didn't know it at the time that he was the man who had us digging up graves, sometimes even after another unit had already come through and dug them up. After they had been dug up a few times, the bodies started coming apart, which made them hard to count. It bothered me that we had to do that; it just didn't make sense to me. McNamara wouldn't have known anyway if we had just estimated. The officers didn't have to do the digging and the counting, so they didn't really care.

What interested me in reading his book was that the day before McNamara's retirement party, the president awarded him the Presidential Medal of Freedom with high honors. This was the biggest oxymoron I had ever heard in my life. On top of that, the military had organized a "full-fledged farewell ceremony in his honor complete with speeches, a military band, an honor guard, an artillery salute, and a flyover with Navy and Air Force jets" (McNamara 316). He was going to make a speech but was so choked up with emotion that he was not able to deliver it. McNamara writes, "I choked back conflicting feelings of pride, gratitude, frustration, sadness, and failure" (McNamara 317). He didn't say he was sorry or ask for forgiveness.

I asked myself how he could even show up to be honored, and how he could accept the Medal of Freedom. I also ask: Could this have been the biggest psychotic disconnect the likes of which anyone has ever seen? This man was responsible, in my opinion, for hundreds of thousands of unnecessary deaths, yet he was so emotionally sensitive he could not deliver a goodbye speech? I would like to think that just maybe he was facing the realization of what he had done, although he does not admit to it, and maybe that was the reason he got choked up.

In fairness, McNamara, near the end, did want the president to stop the war, but it was a feeble attempt. He didn't have the guts to go public or resign.

During the ceremony, a big storm hit with sleet and rain, which cancelled out the flyover and the band, and shorted out the public address system. The ceremony had to be cancelled—kind of makes you wonder. McNamara went on to his next job as president of the World Bank and, I imagine, lived happily ever after.

The third major player was General William Westmoreland. He was a military man whose job it was to wage war. Apparently he didn't care about continuing the slaughter of multiple thousands of people either. Remember, he was the one who recommended the United States take "whatever measures necessary to postpone indefinitely the day of collapse." My take on Westmoreland is that he wanted to keep the war going and make it look like we were making progress so it wouldn't appear like the great general was losing. Generals like to win, you know.

I think in examining the character and values of many world leaders, you will find them to be lacking in humanitarian values. In their rise to power they seem to lack a sensitivity towards poverty and suffering, social justice, and death. That is evident today in America among some of the candidates running for political office. Ironically, these candidates stand tall in their Christian identities.

Years ago I went to one of the 173rd unit reunions. It is the only one I have ever attended. My purpose was to be with my combat brothers for fellowship, getting drunk, and coming away somewhat healed and feeling better about my experiences over there. That was a good purpose, and I did enjoy myself.

I also went because I had a lot of questions, and there were going to be a few high-ranking officers from the brigade attending. Most importantly General Westmoreland himself was going to be the keynote speaker.

Before the ceremony, the general was there for a photo op, dressed in his uniform. It was as if God himself were standing there. I was one of many who walked toward him when it was my turn to shake his hand. I wanted to ask questions, but he said he wasn't taking questions.

There was a presence about him that was eerie. He stood like a statue with very little body movement. He barely spoke, but when he did, there was no affect, no smiling, no facial expressions. He made brief eye contact, but I felt there was no recognition in him of me as an individual. In his eyes, I was just a speck. He wasn't connecting with anybody.

When he gave his speech he said that our unit was the best in Vietnam. When he said that, a roar of applause erupted as we all needed to hear that; we all wanted some form of validation. He then said that the only battle he ever lost was, I think, with CBS, who he took to court because they accused him of lying about the body count and about the war.

At the reunion his speech must have been no longer than thirty seconds, and then he just walked away. What could he have talked about anyway? About a third of the men who did the actual fighting had been killed, mostly because of his ego and pride.

I am surprised he even showed up, because there was no way he could have justified keeping the war going over there or admit we were losing. He didn't seem to have the inner strength to articulate that. Perhaps he sensed no one would have been able to handle that truth. During the war, knowing we could not possibly win, why didn't he just resign and stop the death?

It is an interesting paradox that he possessed the image of a tough general who would never quit. At the same time, I question whether he possessed a weakness of character that would not allow him to make the decision to quit, and I don't suppose I will ever have an answer.

I have no respect for the man. I know generals are supposed to follow orders to fight. But in this obviously impossible situation, I can't believe that this man did not possess the integrity to tell the truth, stand up to the president, and resign. How many thousands of lives would have been spared had he done so? We were not fighting in defense of our own country. If he had been replaced by another general, at least the blood would not be on his hands. In my opinion, that would have made him a real hero and perhaps saved his soul.

Upon my arrival, I tried to talk a reunion director into forming a panel of the older officers who led our unit. I thought it would have been a perfect opportunity to have our questions answered about what the hell was going on during the war. My idea was not well received. In fact, the organizers seemed to guard and protect these officers from anything that might be uncomfortable for them. They were falling all over them.

This was just another example of enlisted men knowing their place. It was the same old awareness of rank, the same response to authority; or perhaps the problem was that we were all suffering from PTSD, mixed feelings, anger and confusion, and didn't have the wherewithal to hold our leaders accountable. Perhaps enlisted vets couldn't think straight enough to go after the truth; possibly we were all in denial.

Looking back on it, I had serious psychological problems and anger of my own. Maybe the officers were also crazy, angry, and depressed. Maybe they had questions for Westmoreland themselves. It seemed to me the reunion was a big gathering of blubbering, drunken, crazy people. It was obvious that I had expected too much from this gathering.

One night, a vet got on the band platform at the bar and yelled that he was going to find out who his real brothers were. He then proceeded to take out a knife and slice his arm. Then he challenged men to come up, cut their arms, and put their wounds against his to become his "blood brother." I wasn't there at the time, and I don't know if anyone followed through; they probably did. Paratroopers were a wild bunch to say the least. It was obvious that this man was making a cry for help.

For years I have had real anger issues about being made a pawn in a great slaughter. I had thought about going after the captain of our company to expose him for leading us into that bloody ambush, taking credit for calling in the air-strikes that saved the company from total annihilation, and then accepting a huge medal for his lie.

After much pondering and struggle I have decided to put the past behind me as much as this is possible. I will not try anymore to get him to make an effort to get my friend a Silver Star, either. Apparently, he changed his phone number and address so I could not find him anymore. He knows the truth and has to live with his conscience. Perhaps that is punishment enough. After this book gets published I will have a better chance of getting my friend a medal.

As for me, I am trying to forgive everyone, including myself, and I hope God forgives me for the taking of life. Hopefully, in the end, my good works will outweigh my bad. In the last half of my life, I have searched to find truth and the meaning of life in order to continue to survive.

When one's soul is damaged as mine is, no matter how hard l work, scars remain. As part of my redemption, I have tried to serve those around me who are struggling, in pain, and less fortunate than I. I have tried to solve problems and address the needs of my community. Through the RV park I worked to create a safe community of mutual respect, with people helping people and truly caring for each other.

I have tried to redeem myself by spending over thirty years immersed in a helping profession, but still I have not done enough.

If this book can improve how the Army operates, if suicide rates start declining, and if it helps other combat veterans understand more about their PTSD, I will feel fulfilled. I hope this book helps them on their journeys to find their own truths.

This is my spiritual message: If veterans can practice love, compassion, and service to others, they will discover the key to healing from or at least to surviving PTSD.

I have the deepest respect for today's military men and women. They are America's cream of the crop. Unlike the Vietnam War, I fully realize we need to protect our country from terrorists. But let's go after the terrorist leaders as we did with Osama bin Laden. We have drones that can fight the war. There is no reason we need to get our troops killed by driving around getting blown up by IEDs, kicking in doors, searching caves, and trying to kill people of little strategic significance, who do not cause much of a threat.

Let's bring the troops home. Let's stop our traditional meddling in the affairs of other countries. Let's stop trying to cram our own brand of democracy and freedom down the throats of other countries. When will we learn we cannot change another country's culture? When will we learn that what is good for our country is not necessarily good for another? When will this country stop the practice of international ethnocentrism and American exceptionalism toward other countries?

I am still a whacked-out vet and continue to struggle with PTSD. I am often an angry and negative person. Like lots of other Vietnam vets I have trust issues and major problems with authority figures. I still have problems that I don't care to talk about. But I am getting better. My wife tells me that she has seen some improvement over the years. In a loving way, she has always been brutally honest with me, so I believe her.

I am getting old, and I need to rest, and I have to find peace with my past in my final years. I have almost forgiven the captain . . . I hope God will forgive me the sins of my past and will look kindly upon the good works of the latter part of my life where I have sought truth and redemption.

This book has been my catharsis. I have a wife, daughter, son, and grandkids who love me. I am a blessed man.

www.ingramcontent.com/pod-product-compliance
Lightning Source LLC
Chambersburg PA
CBHW030252290526
45785CB00001B/64